Alanson Hosmer Phelps

Genealogy and a short Historical Narrative of one Branch of the

Family of George Phelps since the Founding

Alanson Hosmer Phelps

Genealogy and a short Historical Narrative of one Branch of the
Family of George Phelps since the Founding

ISBN/EAN: 9783744729468

Printed in Europe, USA, Canada, Australia, Japan

Cover: Foto ©ninafisch / pixelio.de

More available books at **www.hansebooks.com**

ALANSON HOSMER PHELPS IN 1897

GENEALOGY

And a Short
Historical Narrative
of one Branch
of the

Family of George Phelps

Since the
Founding of the Family
in America by
William and George Phelps
in 1630

EDITED BY
Alanson Hosmer Phelps
SAN FRANCISCO, CAL.
1897

"THEY ONLY DESERVE TO BE REMEMBERED BY POSTERITY WHO TREASURE UP A HISTORY OF THEIR ANCESTORS."

BURKE.

THE PHELPS COAT OF ARMS.

THE SEAL OF THE FAMILY.
(VERY ANTIQUE.)

INTRODUCTION.

In assuming the task of compiling and editing a book relating to the Genealogy of the Phelps Family of our line in America, since the arrival of our ancestors in 1630 to the present date, the editor enters upon the duty with some diffidence.

His chief purpose in doing this has been to collate and transcribe in regular order the material he has accumulated, and in this manner to aid in preserving an authentic history of the family, not alone for his own immediate descendants, but for all others of the name in California, whether they belong to our line or not.

To many this may seem a trivial and unimportant thing to do, but he believes that such a history and genealogy, imperfect and incomplete as it must necessarily be, will prove of great value in many ways in the coming years of the family on the Pacific Coast.

Up to the autumn of 1888, the editor had no positive knowledge whatever of the history of his paternal ancestors any further back than the birth of his grandfather, the second Eliphalet Phelps, and in fact knew but little about him;

he did not even know his great grandfather's name, and only knew in a general way that the latter died when his son, Eliphalet, was a young lad.

In the year above mentioned the editor opened a correspondence with A. T. Servin, Esq., of Lenox, Mass., with the happy result that Mr. Servin was able to furnish him with an authentic and well-written account of the genealogy of his family from the year 1630. The information in this book, covering the genealogy of the family from the coming of the three brothers, William, George and Richard Phelps to America in 1630, down to the birth of the second Eliphalet Phelps, was obtained through the researches of Mr. Servin in old church records in Connecticut and Massachusetts, and from numerous old family records as well.

For a great many years Mr. Servin has been very much interested in the history of the Phelps family, his wife having been a Miss Phelps, and there is no doubt that he has a greater fund of information touching the early history of the family than any other person in the United States.

In addition to the information furnished by Mr. Servin, the editor is under obligation to Miss Mary Bronson Phelps, the third daughter of Rev. Alanson Phelps, for many historical facts which are incorporated in Chapters II, III, IV, V, VI and VII.

The history here recorded since the birth of Grandfather Eliphalet Phelps, has been obtained by the editor from old family records which have been preserved by the children of Grandfather Eliphalet Phelps, to which have been added some legends of the family, which have come down from generation to generation.

With this statement the editor submits the work to his descendants, and to the care of all the descendants of the eight generation, whose names are recorded here, with the request for them sacredly to preserve it, and add to it their own family histories as the years go on.

ALANSON HOSMER PHELPS.

San Francisco, California, 1897.

NOTE.—To any genealogist of the future who may become possessed with a desire to make deeper researches into the history of the general family of Phelps in the United States than the editor has done, he would recommend the following works which may be consulted with advantage, viz.: Stiles' History of Windsor, Conn.; Brown's West Simsbury Connecticut Settlers; Marshall's Grant Ancestry; Strong Genealogy, two volumes; Porter Genealogy; Stiles' Genealogy, and Hinman's Connecticut Settlers, in two volumes, first edition.

CONTENTS.

INTRODUCTION.

OUR LINEAGE.

CHAPTER I..............................The Line of the Family.
CHAPTER II......................William Phelps the Pilgrim.
CHAPTER III.....................George Phelps the Pilgrim.
The First Generation.

CHAPTER IV..Jacob Phelps.
The Second Generation.

CHAPTER V..Jedediah Phelps.
The Third Generation.

CHAPTER VI...Silas Phelps.
The Fourth Generation.

CHAPTER VII..................................Eliphalet Phelps.
The Fifth Generation.

CHAPTER VIII.................................Eliphalet Phelps.
The Sixth Generation.

CHAPTER IX..........The Daughters of Eliphalet Phelps.
CHAPTER X..Asahel Phelps.
The Seventh Generation.

CHAPTER XI.......................................Harvey Phelps.
The Seventh Generation.

CONTENTS—Continued.

CHAPTER XII............ ....Asa Hosmer Phelps.
    The Seventh Generation.

CHAPTER XIII.............................Reuben Phelps.
    The Seventh Generation.

CHAPTER XIV...... ....Alanson Phelps.
    The Seventh Generation.

CHAPTER XV..........The Family of Asa Hosmer Phelps.
    William Sydney Phelps.
    The Eighth Generation.

CHAPTER XIV.......... ....Emma Aurelia Phelps.
    The Eighth Generation.

CHAPTER XVII............ ....Sarah Sophia Phelps.
    The Eighth Generation.

CHAPTER XVIII................Augustus Eliphalet Phelps.
    The Eighth Generation.

CHAPTER XIX......... ....Alanson Hosmer Phelps.
    The Eighth Generation.

CHAPTER XX................... ......Daniel Townsend Phelps.
    The Eighth Generation.

CHAPTER XXI.................A Tradition of the Family.
CHAPTER XXII....Some Reminiscenses of the Family in
    England and America.

CHAPTER XXIII............ ....Conclusion.

OUR LINEAGE.

Turn back for us, relentless Time,
    The records of thy hoary age,
For us unroll thy leaves of scroll:
    Tell us our lineage.

Who was our great progenitor?
    Was he a man of brawn and might?
Beneath what clime, O Sage of Time,
    Did he first see the light.

Was it beneath Italian skies,
    Where liquid vowels outward flow?
Where softly shines amid her vines
    The silv'ry river Po?

Hid in the tomes of obscure lore—
    Dim in the mystery of years,—
Tho' humbly born, yet nobly worn
    The name of WELPHS appears.

Turn back, turn back, O Father Time,
    The revolutions of thy wheel,
The secrets tell which in thee dwell,—
    Thy history reveal.

The centuries e'er roll and roll.
    " Beyond those peaks which limn the skies
Doth Nature's Art—her subtle Art
    Conceal a Paradise?

" Beyond those hills what wonders lie?'
    So spake Italian men of old;
" We will arise, o'er yonder lies
    A land for us foretold."

O'er fen and field, o'er snowy range
    To the rich hills of purple wine,—
To German's land, whose castles stand
    Along the flowing Rhine,

They came with songs and trump of horns,
    And often, down descending years,
In manly pride beside a bride
    A noble GUELPH appears.

Turn back thy book for us, O Time,
    And light on all its pages cast,—
In every line help us divine
    The mysteries of the past.

The centuries sweep on and roll.
    Across a surging, spiteful sea
Which rears and roars along the shores
    Of Britain's destiny,

Appeared a man of martial form,
    To bring that land enduring fame;
With fierce desire, and eye of fire
    William, the Conqueror, came.

"I yield thee homage true," spake one,
    "And when thy flag on Britain stands,
Bold Prince and great, I place my fate
    Within thy kingly hands."

The King was gracious, and he smiled.
    "Fetch me the book," unto a page,
"In letters clear, inscribe it here,
    The PHYLLYPPS lineage."

Go forward now with us, O Time,
    As we go on our pilgrimage
Thro' ocean gates, where grandly waits,
    A richer heritage.

The centuries roll on and roll
    Until the Pope's most holy eyes,
See in the air of Britain fair
    The Puritans arise.

Dire persecutions on them fall;
  "We must depart—our homes forsake—
An Empire found, on nobler ground,
  For our Redeemer's sake."

"MARY & JOHN" the good ship, spreads
  Her sails to meet the luring breeze,
Her fabric bears both hope and fears
  Across tempestuous seas.

At morn they rise and bend in prayer,
  At evening sing "We seek a home,"
While on the decks, the ocean flecks,
  Its lace-like fringe of foam.

The irksome sea-life wearies all;
  They peer and watch, they yearn for land,
With psalms and praise they grace the days
  While sailing in God's hand.

At last, at last, from masthead comes
  A voice resounding shrill and clear;
"Land! land! I see upon our lee!
  The land! the land is near!"

All night the ship wears slowly on,
  Until the breaking of the day.
They warp and weave, her anchors heave,
  In Massachusetts Bay.

They view a land inert, untried,
  Of richness unsurpassed by Ind;
Veiled in deep veins, were golden grains
  Ere Eve with Satan sinned.

In solitude and loneliness
  The forest comes to meet the sea;
No homes are there—the forest air
  Waits for the homes to be.

The Puritans at once debark,
  While gladly every seaman helps,
When to that shore, the pinnace bore,
  The Pilgrim WILLIAM PHELPS.

His faltering pen the bard resigns,
   And leaves the records he has found
Of WELPHS, of GUELPHS, PHYLLYPPS and
      PHELPS.
   Of lineage renowned.

Roll on, roll on, O ceaseless Time
   Thy centuries from age to age,
While every PHELPS, with ardor helps
   Preserve his lineage.

—ALANSON HOSMER PHELPS.

TO 'SCAPE THE TYRANNY OF HATE
  OUR PILGRIM FATHERS CAME,
AND THROUGH THE WILDERNESS THEY STEPT
  TO EVERLASTING FAME.

GENEALOGY OF THE PHELPS FAMILY.

CHAPTER I.

THE LINE OF THE FAMILY.

Three brothers named William, George and Richard Phelps, emigrated from England and landed at Dorchester, near Boston, Massachusetts, in 1630, coming on the ship "Mary & John."

Of these three brothers only two were the founders of the family in America, as Richard soon after arriving in Dorchester went on a voyage to the West Indies, from which he never returned, and there is no knowledge as to his fate.

Of the two brothers who remained in Dorchester, the youngest, George Phelps, was our ancestor, and is called the First Generation in this Record.

First Generation—George Phelps, the Pilgrim.

Second Generation—Jacob Phelps, the 6th child of George Phelps.

Third Generation—Jedediah Phelps, the 7th child of Jacob Phelps.

Fourth Generation—Silas Phelps, the 5th

child of Jedediah Phelps.

Fifth Generation—Eliphalet Phelps, the 1st child of Silas Phelps.

Sixth Generation—Eliphalet Phelps, the 1st child of Eliphalet Phelps.

Seventh Generation—Asa Hosmer Phelps, the 4th child of Eliphalet Phelps.

Eighth Generation — Alanson Hosmer Phelps, the 5th child of Asa Hosmer Phelps.

Ninth Generation—Albert Alanson Phelps, the 1st child of Alanson Hosmer Phelps.

Ninth Generation—Roger Sherman Phelps, the 3d child of Alanson Hosmer Phelps.

CHAPTER II.

WILLIAM PHELPS THE PILGRIM.

William, George and Richard Phelps, brothers, were born in Tewksbury, Gloucestershire, England, where descendants of the family still reside.

William Phelps was born August 19th, 1599. He removed from Tewksbury, (date unknown,) to Somerset or Dorsetshire, where he married Elizabeth ————, by whom he had five children.

Their children were:

First. William Phelps, born in 1620, married Isabel Wilson, June 4th, 1645.

Married second time Sarah Phinney.

Second. Sarah Phelps, born in 1623, married William Wade, June 9th, 1658.

Third. Samuel Phelps, born in 1625, married Sarah Griswold, November 10, 1650.

Fourth. Nathaniel Phelps, born in 1627, married Elizabeth Copley, September 17th, 1650.

Fifth. Joseph Phelps, born in 1629, married Hannah Newton, September 20, 1660.

These were the children of William Phelps the Pilgrim, all born in England by his wife Elizabeth. After her death, of which we can find no record, he married for his second wife Mary Dover, by whom he had two children. They were married at Windsor, Conn., (no date). She is said to have been a fellow passenger in the "Mary & John."

Their children were:

First. Timothy Phelps, born in Windsor, Conn., August 1639, married Mary Griswold.

Second. Mary Phelps, born in Windsor, Conn., March 1644, married Thomas Barber.

The following is taken from old family records and letters:

"Auld William Phyllypps came to America in the ship 'Mary & John,' Captain John Squeb, which sailed from Plymouth, England, on March 20th, 1630 (Old Style). It was a ship of 400 tons burthen and brought over 140 passengers from the Southern Counties of England, who landed at Dorchester, on the Coast of Massachusetts on the 30th day of May, 1630."

They were Pilgrims and were driven from their fatherland, not by earthly want, not by love of adventure, but they came to seek a land where they could worship God in accordance with the dictates of their own consciences. They had been organized into a church at Plymouth, and made choice of the Rev. John Warham as pastor, and the Rev. Mr. Maverick as teacher. Mr. Clapp, one of the passengers, writes: "We came by the good hand of the Lord through the deep comfortably, having preaching and expounding of the Word every day for seventy days by our ministers—a ten-weeks' protracted meeting."

The following is taken from "Stiles' History of Windsor, Conn.:"

"Auld William Phyllypps was one of the first settlers and grantees of land at Dorchester. He applied for Freemanship October 30th, 1634, and came to Windsor in the spring of 1636, whither his brother George is understood to have preceded him. He came to Dorchester (near Boston) in 1630, with the Rev. Mr. Warham, of whose church he, with his wife Elizabeth, were members. The superfluous letters in the name were dropped during the reign of Edward the VI." He was a gentleman of opulence, leaving a large estate in Staffordshire, England, which, of course, reverted to the British Crown.

William and George Phelps resided in Dorchester up to 1635.

During these five years their names were often referred to in the "Documentary History of Massachusetts Colony" as "Representative Men."

In the fall of 1635, with others, they removed to the founding of the town of Windsor, in the beautiful valley of the Connecticut.

Here William became one of the most prominent and highly respected men of the colony. He was a member of the first court held in Connecticut in 1636; also of the court of 1637, which declared war with the Pequots;

a Magistrate (Senator) from 1638 until the close of 1642.

In 1643 he was Foreman of the first Grand Jury; Deputy in 1645, '46, '47, '48, '49, '51 and '52. In 1658 he was again made Magistrate, which office he held for four years after. In 1661, in company with Mr. Wells of Hartford, they were appointed a committee on *Lying*. He was an excellent, pious and upright man in public and private life, and was a pillar of both Church and State. In those days the title of "Mister" was given to only a few, and was considered a mark of respect and honor; it was always given to him.

He served twenty sessions in all as a Magistrate. He was married twice and had seven children. His second wife, Mary Dover, died November 27th, 1675.

He lived about thirty-seven years in Windsor, and died there on July 14th, 1672, aged 73 years.

With many other pilgrim fathers he helped to lay broad and deep the foundations of this now ocean-bound Republic; and his grave, although searched for, is unknown to this day.

Extract from an old letter, the writer of which is unknown:

"I saw the place where 'Auld William' lived. The house was standing until a few years ago. Another dwelling, not far off, is occupied by one of his descendants on the same ground. It is still called 'Phelps' Hill.' The view is fine and extensive. An old elm tree stands on the opposite side of the public road, whose branches extend across, touching the grass, and forms a complete bower."

From a letter of William Calvin Phelps of the seventh generation, written to Oliver Seymour Phelps of Portland, Oregon, dated at Winterset, Iowa, July 1st, 1881, the following extract is made:

"You made inquiry about the piece of an ancient bedstead which I had obtained. According to the tradition, to which I am indebted for all my information respecting it, it was brought to Massachusetts from old England in 1630, and then to Windsor, Conn., by William Phelps, in 1635.

"He purchased a large tract of land three miles in length (of "Sehat" a Pauquanick Sachem, for four "trucking coats," in 1635, though this Indian deed bears date March 31st, 1665) in Windsor, in what is now Poquonnuck Society, and built a house on a little knoll about half way from the Farmington river to the present road to Rainbow.

"The cellar of his house is still pointed out by those of his descendants that remain, one or more branches of whom settled near him, and through them have come down in unbroken line, the bedstead, a large chest, a pair of tongs and a coat of arms.

"The coat of arms was given to Launcelot Manfield and came into his family by marriage.

Hiram Phelps, a cousin of my father, has had them in his possession, till his death, eight or ten years ago, since about 1800.

"The coat of arms and the tongs are now in the possession of his daughter, Mrs. Eliza Kinney, of Winsted, who prizes them highly as relics. The foot rail of the bedstead was all I could find of it. The old chest, though in a rickety condition, is nearly whole, and remains in the old home, where it has been from time long ago."

It can be truthfully said of these Phelps brothers and their descendants that they are a royal family—producing statesmen, princely merchants, famous inventors, literary and poetical men, and men of liberal and philthropic ideas, comparing favorably with any of the first families of America. President Hayes, on his maternal side, was a Phelps, and the United States Minister to the Court of St. James under President Cleveland's first term, the Hon. E. J. Phelps of Vermont, is a descendant of William.

Many other men of both branches have served as senators, governors, and representatives, with honor and distinction.

Of princely merchants of the line of George Phelps, we have Anson G. Phelps, Royal Phelps, John Jay Phelps and many others of this line. The history of the family shows that it can be traced as a liberal family, and always for freedom, from the Welphs of Italy from the 6th to the 9th century. Later in the Guelphs of Germany from the 9th to the 11th century, and from there to England from the 11th to the 12th century, probably with William the Conqueror, where we identify them as respectable land-holders, as Phellepps, Philips, Phyllypps, Phelpes and finally as now Phelps.

William Phelps of this record was born in Tewksbury, August 19th, 1599.

He was the son of William Phelps, born in Tewksbury, August 14th, 1560. He was Bailiff (Mayor) there in 1607.

Parish Register Entry: "Lent, 1599. I graunted a license to William Phelpes, being extremely sicke, to eat fleshe, which license to endure no longer tyme than during his sicknes."

RI CURTEIS, *Curate of Tewksburie.*

For the benefit of all who may desire to learn something of the ancestry of the family in England, before the emigration of William Phelps the Pilgrim and his two brothers to America, the editor inserts here the record of the family of William Phelps, the father of William Phelps the Pilgrim.

William Phelps, born in Tewksbury, August 14th, 1560. Married. Name of wife and date of marriage unknown.

Their children were:

First. Mary Phelps, born September 4th, 1587.

Second. Dorothy Phelps, born February 28th, 1595.

Third. William Phelps, born August 19th, 1599.

Fourth. James Phelps, born July 14th, 1601.

Fifth. Elizabeth Phelps, born May 9th, 1603.

Sixth. George Phelps, born —— 1605.

Seventh. Richard Phelps, born December 26th, 1619.

William Phelps, the father of William Phelps the Pilgrim, was the son of James Phelps, born in Tewksbury about the year 1520, where, beneath the shadow of the venerable Abbey Church, built by Fitz Hamon, A. D. 1105, many of the Phelps family lie interred.

Matthew Grant, the founder of the family of General U. S. Grant, in America, came to America in the ship "Mary & John" and landed at Dorchester, Massachusetts, in May, 1630. With many others he went to Connecticut and assisted in founding the town of Windsor in 1635, probably with our ancestors, William and George Phelps.*

---

*Personal Memoirs of U. S. Grant, vol. I, pages 17 and 18.

CHAPTER III.

GEORGE PHELPS THE PILGRIM.

George Phelps, the sixth child of William Phelps, of Tewksbury, England, was born in Tewksbury in 1605. With his brothers, William and Richard, he came to America and landed at Dorchester, Mass., in May, 1630.

In the fall of 1635 he removed to the founding of the town of Windsor, Conn. He married twice, his first wife being Philura Randall, daughter of Philip Randall (date of marriage given as 1637).

By her he had five children. She was born in England, and died April 20th, 1648.

The children were:

First. Isaac Phelps, born in Windsor, Conn., August 20th, 1638.

Second. Abraham Phelps, born in Windsor, Conn., January 22d, 1642. He was adopted by his cousin, Abraham Randall.

Third. —— ——, born in Windsor, Conn., 1647.

Fourth. —— ——, born in Windsor, Conn., 1647.

Fifth. Joseph Phelps, born in Windsor,

Conn., June 24th, 1647. Married Mary, daughter of John and Mary Porter.

The second wife of George Phelps was a widow when he espoused her, a Mrs. Frances Dewey—her maiden name unknown. By her he had three children.

First. Jacob Phelps (his sixth child), born in Windsor, Conn., February 7th, 1650.

Second. John Phelps (his seventh child), born in Windsor, Conn., February 15th, 1651.

Third. Nathaniel Phelps (eighth child), born in Windsor, Conn., December 9th, 1653.

By the Colonial Records it appears that George Phelps was a representative man in the colony from 1658 to 1663. Says "Trumbull's History of Connecticut:" "He held the office of Magistrate, or as then called, 'Assistant.'"

This then constituted the upper house of the Assembly, and at that time was the Superior Court of the colony. In 1676 he removed with his family and his second wife to Westfield, Mass., a new town set off from Springfield, Mass. Here he died July 9th, 1678.

CHAPTER IV.

JACOB PHELPS, THE SECOND GENERATION.

Jacob Phelps, the sixth child of George Phelps, and the first by his second wife, was born in Windsor, Conn., February 7th, 1650.

He married Dorothy Ingersol, May 2d, 1672. She was born in Hartford, Conn., in 1654, and was the second child of John and Dorothy (Lord) Ingersol, who settled in Westfield about the time the Phelps family moved there. Jacob Phelps removed to Westfield with his father, where he settled, and he died there on the 6th of October, 1689, aged 39 years.

His children were:

First. Dorothy Phelps, born in Westfield, Mass., October, 1673, and died February, 1674.

Second. Dorothy Phelps, born in Westfield, Mass., May 20th, 1675. Married Edward Kibbie.

Third. Hannah Phelps, born in Westfield, Mass., November 16th, 1677. Married John Kibbie.

Fourth. Israel Phelps, born in Westfield, Mass., April 3d, 1681.

Fifth. Benjamin Phelps, born in Westfield, Mass., January 8th, 1683.

Sixth. Joseph Phelps, born in Westfield, Mass., August 5th, 1686.

Seventh. Jedediah Phelps, born in Westfield, Mass., December 7th, 1688.

Of the daughters, Dorothy second, and Hannah married brothers.

The four sons all settled in Lebanon, Conn. Israel Phelps purchased land there January 30th, 1702, and the other brothers soon after. He lived there but a short time, when he removed to Enfield, Conn.

There are full records of his descendants. Benjamin settled in Mansfield, Conn., about 1710, where some of his descendants still reside.

Joseph Phelps lived and died in Lebanon, Conn.

CHAPTER V.

JEDEDIAH PHELPS, THE THIRD GENERATION.

Jedediah Phelps was the seventh child of Jacob and Dorothy (Ingersol) Phelps, and was born in Westfield, Conn., December 7th, 1688.

He married Elizabeth Janes (no date of marriage given). She was the daughter of Abel Janes and Mary (Judd) Janes.

She died in Lebanon, Conn., April 10th, 1757.

Jedediah Phelps settled in Lebanon early in life with his three brothers, where we find many transactions in the purchase and sale of real estate by these brothers. The first record found of Jedediah Phelps is that Joseph and Jedediah Phelps (the latter then about 21 years old) purchased of Joseph Dewey for the sum of 39 pounds 10 shillings current money of New England, a parcel of land containing seventy acres, with a common right of thirty-five acres, the other tract containing five acres (the house lot).

Deed dated May 9th, 1709, recorded Vol. 2, page 132.

He bought of Abel Janes (his father-in-law) several parcels of land—one of forty acres, one of five and one of eight acres; deed dated January 17th, 1717; recorded Vol. 3, page 61, with several other transactions. He died in Lebanon, Conn., February 13th, 1752.

His children were:

First. Elizabeth Phelps, born in Lebanon, Conn., December 3d, 1709.

Second. Abigail Phelps, born in Lebanon, Conn., November 4th, 1710. Married first T. Henry.

Third. Jacob Phelps, born in Lebanon, Conn., April 16th 1713.

Fourth. Paul Phelps, born in Lebanon, Conn., April 25th, 1717.

Fifth. Silas Phelps, born in Lebanon, Conn., January 17th, 1720.

Sixth. Jemima Phelps, born in Lebanon, Conn., January 26, 1724, died July 5, 1739.

Seventh. Lucy Phelps, born in Lebanon, Conn. (no date given). Married John Lyman.

Eighth. Jedediah Phelps, born in Lebanon, Conn., June 20th, 1727.

Ninth. Eleanor Phelps, born in Lebanon, Conn., (no date given). Married —— Crocker.

Of this family Jacob died in 1751. He had four children in all—all daughters. Paul had several daughters, and only one son who died in 1752.

Jedediah had two children who died young. He died in 1752.

It would appear that all the children of Jedediah Phelps except his son Silas, and Lucy or

Lucia, and Eleanor, who married —— Crocker, were all the children living at the time of their father's death.

From Probate Court Records in 1754, Vol. 5, page 89, it would appear that the estate of Jedediah Phelps was divided between his daughters Lucia, Eleanor Crocker and Silas.

CHAPTER VI.

SILAS PHELPS, THE FOURTH GENERATION.

Silas Phelps, the fifth child of Jedediah and Elizabeth (Janes) Phelps, was born in Lebanon, Conn., January 27th, 1720. Married Hannah Dewey Dec. 22d, 1742. She was the daughter of William Dewey, born May 14th, 1723, and died at Lebanon, Conn., October 24th, 1785, aged 62 years.

Silas Phelps lived on his father's homestead. We find several records of purchases of real estate. In 1787 it appears that he became involved in litigation, and several executions were levied against his estate—one in favor of Thomas Brattle of Boston, for 193 pounds, 13 shillings and 9 pence, November 6th, 1787, see Vol. 15 page 21. Also one in favor of William Williams for 21 pounds, 13 shillings and 7 pence, Dec. 19, 1787, Vol. 15 page 35.

About 1790 he removed with his sons Silas and Jedediah to Oneida County, New York, where other records of his family say he died, in 1816, aged 96 years. Reference is made to this family in the "Annals of Oneida County, N. Y."

His children were:

First. Eliphalet Phelps, born in Lebanon, Conn., November 5th, 1745.

Second. Anna Phelps, born in Lebanon, Conn., April 27th, 1747.

Third. Silas Phelps, born in Lebanon, Conn., May 15th, 1751.

Fourth. Jedediah Phelps, born in Lebanon, Conn., April 23d, 1753.

Fifth. Jacob Phelps, born in Lebanon, Conn., January 30th, 1755.

Sixth. Joseph Phelps, born in Lebanon, Conn., May 27th, 1758.

Of this family, Silas, Jedediah and Joseph settled in Oneida County, New York, their father Silas going with them there, where he died in 1816 as previously stated.

CHAPTER VII.

ELIPHALET PHELPS, THE FIFTH GENERATION.

Eliphalet Phelps was the first child of Silas and Hannah (Dewey) Phelps, and was born in Windsor, Conn., November 5th, 1743; baptized December 18th, 1743; married Mehitable Hyde, daughter of Bezaliel and Mehitable (Porter) Hyde (no date of marriage given). Eliphalet Phelps settled in Lebanon on the homestead of his father, where he had two children.

His children were:

First. Eliphalet Phelps, born in Lebanon, Conn., May 11th, 1765.

Second. Hannah Phelps, born in Lebanon, Conn., May 11th, 1765.

Eliphalet and Hannah were twins.

In the church records it appears that Eliphalet and Hannah Phelps were baptized November 24th, 1765.

At what date Eliphalet Phelps died our records fail to show.

The above Hannah Phelps married Josiah Woodward. They settled in New York State, and had two children, Benjamin and Lucy Woodward.

Lucy Woodward married Captain Asa

Hosmer, by whom she had two daughters and one son.

Her first daughter, Lucy Woodward Hosmer, married James Perkins.

Her second daughter, Sophia Eliza Hosmer, married Ludyah Robinson, from whom are descended the Robinson family of New York and San Francisco.

"Aunt Hosmer," as she was affectionately called by the children of Eliphalet Phelps of the sixth generation, was a woman very much beloved by them, and by her marriage to Captain Asa Hosmer, the names of Asa and Asa Hosmer were introduced into the family of the seventh generation.

The great-grandfather of the editor, Eliphalet Phelps of the fifth generation, served in the war of the revolution, serving one month—as quite common at that time, when at any emergency men were enlisted to serve for such length of time as might be necessary—some only for three or six days, others for one or two months, as the case might be. He served in the Eighteenth Regiment of Connecticut Militia, Captain Forward's company.

This regiment was detailed for service in New York State from August 24th, 1776, to September 24th, 1776.

His two brothers, Silas and Jedediah Phelps, also served in the revolutionary army. Silas was in the Seventeenth Continental; was a sergeant, also a pensioner, and the name of Jedediah is found in the Lexington alarm list.

The Register, published by the State of Connecticut containing the names of all her citizens who served in the revolution, contains the names of *seventy-six soldiers of the name of Phelps*, who enlisted from Connecticut alone.

As Eliphalet Phelps is the direct ancestor of all the children of our line, we, the descendants of Eliphalet Phelps of the fifth generation, are eligible to membership in the "Societies of the Sons and Daughters of the American Revolution."

We are also eligible to join the "Society of Colonial Wars," through the following ancestors:

George Phelps, member of the Hartford Company, First Troop, 1658; member of "Council of Ten."

Hugh Calkins, 1650 and '51, deputy to the General Court of Massachusetts Bay.

Abel Janes, soldier in "Falls Fight," 1676.

Nathaniel Porter, member of army in expedition against Canada, 1708 and '9, and died at Fort Ann, Washington county, New York.

CHAPTER VIII.

ELIPHALET PHELPS, THE SIXTH GENERATION.

Eliphalet Phelps was the first child and only son of Eliphalet and Mehitable (Hyde) Phelps, and was born in Lebanon, Conn., May 11th, 1765.

He married Mehitable Dodge, daughter of Bezaleil and Mehitable (Porter) Dodge, born in Lebanon, Conn., December 2d, 1766.

Eliphalet Phelps removed from Lebanon to New Marlboro, Mass., but the exact year he made the change in his residence is now unknown, but it is supposed to have been about the year 1790, possibly a few years later.

By his one wife, Mehitable Dodge, he had fourteen children, of whom two died in infancy, and twelve lived to grow to manhood and womanhood.

At what particular places they were respectively born is now uncertain, but as it is supposed that he moved to New Marlboro in 1790, all except Hannah, his eldest child, were born in New Marlboro.

Alanson Phelps, the thirteenth child of the family, has left on record the fact that he was born in New Marlboro, Mass.

Eliphalet Phelps emigrated from Massachusetts to the Western Reserve, in the northeastern part of Ohio, probably in the year 1818, and brought with him his wife and all of his living children, so far as known, with the exception of three—Asahel, Asa Hosmer and the second Aurelia.

From a letter received from C. L. Wilcox, Esq., of West Williamsfield, Ashtabula County, Ohio, by the editor, dated May 4th, 1893, regarding the date of Grandfather Phelps' arrival in Ohio, we learn as follows:

"Your favor of April 5th was duly received. I have delayed my reply thus long, hoping to be able to furnish you something definite as to the date of your Grandfather Phelps' arrival in Wayne. Thus far I have found no person or records to show for a certainty such date.

"The old records of the First Congregational Church of Wayne and Williamsfield (which are in my possession), organized in 1816, show that your grandfather joined this society in 1818, at the meeting on the 11th day of December, 1818. This would almost seem to fix the date of his arrival sometime during the season of that year, as people acted promptly in those days, especially in religious matters."

At that time that part of Ohio was a comparative wilderness, the township of Wayne, Ashtabula County, having been first settled by white men in 1803. When first opened to settlement by white men, that country was an unbroken forest for hundreds of miles, commencing probably in the eastern part of the State of New York and extending westward to the verge of the western part of the State of Indiana.

By trade Grandfather Phelps was a blacksmith, and for many years he carried on that business after his arrival in Ohio, and as long as he was able to follow the occupation. In those days people did not have the convenient kitchen utensils which we have now, and they had to depend upon their local artisans to supply them with necessary articles, such as butcher knives, forks, broiling irons, pot hooks, &c. He was very expert in making such light and useful articles, and during the latter years of his life he used to make a great many, which he disposed of to his friends and customers in the towns around. There are a few samples of his work still preserved in our family.

As stated above, the children of Eliphalet and Mehitable Phelps were fourteen. The following are the names of the fourteen children, with the dates of the birth and death of each of them:

First. Hannah Phelps, born March 12th, 1789, died August 16th, 1828.

Second. Asahel Phelps, born March 16th, 1791, died March 12th, 1844.

Third. Harvey Phelps, born August 19th, 1793, died August 16th, 1853.

Fourth. Asa Hosmer Phelps, born April 20th, 1795, died December 14th, 1835.

Fifth. Reuben Phelps, born February 27th, 1797, died March 3d, 1860.

Sixth, Harriet Phelps, born February 20th, 1799, died November 24th, 1852.

Seventh. Melinda Phelps, born October 7th, 1801, died December 14th, 1842.

Eighth. Dyantha Phelps, born November 2d, 1804, died August 16th, 1828.

Ninth. Aurelia Phelps, born November 28th, 1804, died April —, 1805.

Tenth. Aurelia Phelps second, born March 22d, 1806, died February 19th, 1880.

Eleventh. Mary Porter Phelps, born November 21, 1808, died September 15th, 1828.

Twelfth. Alanson Woodward Phelps, born June —, 1810, died October 10th, 1810.

Thirteenth. Alanson Phelps, born February 10th, 1812, died November 5th, 1889.

Fourteenth. Ann Eliza Phelps, born December 14th, 1814, died April 30th, 1840.

The following are the marriages of the children of Eliphalet and Mehitable (Dodge) Phelps:

Hannah Phelps married Harvey Walter in New Marlboro, Mass., December —, 1813.

Asahel Phelps married Rhoda Norton in New Marlboro, Mass., December 15th, 1817.

Asa Hosmer Phelps married Margery McCoun, on Long Island, N. Y., July 21st, 1819.

Harvey Phelps married Betsy Meacham in Ohio, November 9th, 1820.

Reuben Phelps married Olive Leanord in Ohio, February 4th, 1819.

Melinda Phelps married Gamaliel Wilcox in Ohio, April 18th, 1825.

Dyantha Phelps married Pliny Case in Ohio, February —, 1825.

Aurelia Phelps second, married Pliny Case in Ohio, June 19th, 1827.

Mary Porter Phelps married Linus H. Jones in Ohio, November 8th, 1827.

Alanson Phelps married Mary Ann Bronson in Ohio, August 31st, 1841.

Alanson Phelps married Jane Eliza Ensworth in Connecticut, September 29th, 1859.

Ann Eliza Phelps married Dryden Creesy in Ohio, November 20th, 1834.

Grandfather was a religious man, who feared God and taught his children the faith of Jesus Christ. He and his family were Congregationalists, with perhaps two or three exceptions, and, so far as the writer is aware, all of his children, with one exception, were church members.

The church referred to in the extract copied from the letter of Mr. Wilcox already mentioned, was located in the eastern part of the town of Wayne, and was one of the earliest churches, if not the very earliest church, organized in that town. This edifice had a *bell*, one of the first churches in all that part of Ohio to secure a bell with which to call the people to worship.

Owing to a change in the population of the town as it grew older and larger, and to the establishment of other churches nearer the center of the town, the organization that used to worship in this building was finally disbanded, and the old meeting-house many years ago was remodeled into a dwelling house, still standing, at last accounts.

In the old burying-ground attached to this church—which is still preserved and cared for—rest the remains of Grandfather and Grandmother Phelps, Aunt Harriet, Aunt Malinda, Aunt Mary Porter and others of the family, whom the writer is now unable to name.

Many years ago, Uncle Alanson Phelps erected a plain marble headstone over the remains of his father and mother. The stone is of double width, and the style and inscription upon it are as delineated in the sketch on the following page:

OUR PARENTS.

ELIPHALET PHELPS MAHITABEL PHELPS

DIED DIED

March 10, 1842. January 22, 1840.

They Taught Us To Love Jesus

———

Their Children Arise Up And Call
Them Blessed.

———

This Stone Is Erected By Their
Youngest Son.

DO THEY REMEMBER US?

Above these silent shrines of sacred dust
   Let Palms arise—let flowers of every form
   Adorn these lowly mounds with colors warm,
And blend, with earthly grief, a heavenly trust.

Do those who sleep, in spirit see us here?
   From out the depths of the ethereal skies,
   Do they look down with sympathizing eyes
Upon us, as we struggle onward here?

Do they remember us where life is love?
   In that pure life—in that celestial sphere
   Do they remember our communion here?
We know they do love us, for God is love.

Were it God's Will, would they return again
   And enter all this field of worldly strife,
   That fills the measure of this mortal life,
To earn its fruit—its recompense of pain?

We ask these queries, yet no answers come,
   For God hath closed the high and pearly Gate
   And we must linger on, and wait and wait
Until He kindly calls, "My child, come home."

Grandfather Eliphalet Phelps was a man of medium height, about 5 feet 8 or 9 inches tall, as the writer remembers him, of stout build, of a light and florid complexion, and must have weighed in his prime from 180 to 200 pounds. The writer went to Ohio to live with his Aunt Aurelia (Phelps) Case, and to be brought up by her, arriving there in his sixth year—the year of 1837—and he well remembers not only his paternal grandparents, but many of his uncles and aunts.

Grandfather died in his great arm-chair before the fire in the house of his daughter Malinda (Phelps) Wilcox. Grandmother Phelps was a large and tall woman, and of a dark complexion.

There used to be stories extant in Ohio relating to the peculiarities of Eliphalet Phelps in reference to the rapidity with which he ate his meals. In those days people had to live in a primitive way, and had to eat what they could raise on their farms.

Among other dishes much affected was the homely but nutritious dish of "mush and milk."

Of this dish it was said of Eliphalet Phelps, "That he could eat a bowl of mush and milk with a spoon quicker than it could be emptied in any other way."

CHAPTER IX.

THE DAUGHTERS OF ELIPHALET PHELPS.

Hannah Phelps, the first child of Eliphalet and Mehitable Phelps, was born (probably) in Lebanon, Conn., March 12th, 1789.

The record says that she married Harvey Walter in 1813. At this very early date she must have been married in Massachusetts, and the opinion of the writer is that she accompanied her husband soon after to the then far away wilds of Ohio, preceding the family of her father, possibly by two or three years, and it may have been through her influence that the family of her father was induced to emigrate to Ohio.

Her husband settled on a farm one mile and a half south of the centre of the town of Wayne, Ashtabula County.

By him she had two daughters, named Cornelia and Aurilla.

There is but little information obtainable regarding this aunt, and yet we may infer that her life at that period in the history of Ohio was a hard one—a pioneer life—as the place where her husband commenced to make a home was in a dense and heavy forest of trees which had to be cut down and burned up before a crop of any kind could be raised upon the land. The struggle to live must have been a hard one, and her fortitude must have been great to have withstood the toil of that early pioneer life. She died in Wayne, August 28th, 1828.

Cornelia Walter married a man by the name of Collins Jennings.

They lived together for a few years, and had one or two daughters.

One day Mr. Jennings left his home and was never seen or heard of afterwards. What became of him was never known.

Aurilla Walter married a man by the name of Lamb, by whom she had three or four children—all boys—the last two being a pair of twins.

Soon after their birth Aurilla died.

Harriet Phelps, the sixth child and second daughter of Eliphalet and Mehitable (Dodge) Phelps was born in New Marlboro, Mass., February 20th, 1799. Her early life was passed in her native State, and she accompanied her parents to Ohio when they went to that State. At the age of about twenty years she had the misfortune to lose one of her limbs from the effects of a white swelling on the knee, and ever afterwards she walked on crutches, as at that early date the art of making useful cork limbs had not reached the perfection that it now has. Although afflicted in this serious manner, she always maintained a genial and cheerful disposition, and was a most accomplished companion and conversationalist, having more real intellectual ability than any other daughter of Grandfather Phelps, so far as the editor's knowledge extends.

She early learned the tailoring trade, and was an expert artist in that business. She could take a piece of broadcloth and cut, make and press a full suit of clothes for a gentleman, and fit him in good style, as well as any man tailor of those days.

She was well and favorably known in all the towns around where she lived, and she used to sew for many of the best families every year, going to their houses and spending from one week to a month at a time, and continued to do so as long as her health and strength permitted.

In her religious belief she was an ardent and enthusiastic Christian of the old New England Puritan school of practice, believing most thoroughly in the sins of card-playing and dancing, and in keeping the Sabbath day in a very strict manner. I remember her well, as I was in my twenty-first year when she passed to the higher life.

She was a very warm and affectionate sister to her youngest brother, Alanson Phelps, and it was through her assistance that he was enabled to obtain a collegiate education, and no doubt it was also through her influence that he finally decided to enter the Christian ministry.

For many years after the death of her parents she made her home with her sister, Aurelia

Case, and she died at the house of the latter in Greene, Trumbull county, Ohio, in November, 1852. Her remains were taken to the town of Wayne, where the funeral services were held, and she was buried in the old burying-ground already mentioned, and was laid to rest beside her father and mother, and her numerous relatives who are sleeping there. She was a woman any man might be proud to call his aunt. She was always desirous that I should live an upright and honest life, and always taught me lessons of strict morality and integrity.

It is a pleasure to me after the silence of the many years that have passed since she died to lay this little chaplet of affection on her tomb. There is a small, white marble headstone standing over her grave, which was erected by her brother-in-law, Linus H. Jones, who was always an ardent and warm friend of the Phelps family, because of the love he cherished for his first wife, Mary Porter Phelps, and he was always a friend indeed to Aunt Harriet.

The stone he erected is a plain marble slab, is in the form delineated on the opposite page, and has an inscription as copied thereon:

In the possession of the editor is an old letter written by Harriet Phelps to her sister, Aurelia Case, dated Oberlin, Ohio, May 12th, 1841, an extract from which is copied below to show the beautiful character of her mind. The chirography is of the finest and most delicate order, and yet of a clear and flowing style:

OUR FRIEND.

MISS HARRIET PHELPS

DIED

November 24, 1852.

Aged 54 Years.

———

A Daughter's Heart
A Sister's Love
A Light On Earth
Her Crown Above.

———

Hers Was Gold Tried In The Fire.

"Dear Sister Case:

Your letter should have been answered, before, but as I have time to write but seldom, will not waste it in useless apologies.

I will take up the subjects of your letter in their order.

You speak of dear father as very feeble, and probably near death.

I *love* my dear father, as you well know; but if, as you say, he is stretching the wings of faith, and waiting with earnest desire to depart, let him *go*, my dear sister; and the Lord prepare us to follow him.

The sooner he is introduced into that blest society, the better, if it be the will of the Lord. I should love to see my dear father once more, but the Lord has brought me to this place, and my beloved relatives are some one hundred, and some several hundreds of miles from me, and yet I want no good thing, but feel that 'all is well.'

If the Lord should call away every dear relative of mine that remains on earth, I shall not want a friend while Jesus lives.

And if He first prepares my beloved friends, and then takes them to His bosom, I will praise His name forever. I do not want to see my dear father die! I do not want to see him in his coffin!

My very soul died within me when I saw my beloved mother there, and yet there was not a single moment in which I was not perfectly willing the Lord should take her to Himself. But she was my *mother!*

I had no other, nor would I have. 'But the Lord liveth, and blessed be my Rock.' Ah! here is an unfailing friend. And then I am surrounded with other friends, the most valuable and lovely. Yes; relatives, 'for whosoever doeth the Will of my Father which is in heaven, the same is my *brother*, and *sister*, and *mother*.' O blessed relationship to the most noble family, in earth and heaven. You say you 'want to feel entire submission.' *Do* you not? Can the Lord make any mistakes? You answer 'No.' Then let Him do what He will. You say you were '*overwhelmed* with sorrow at the prospect of being left alone.' I think I can truly say nothing *overwhelms* me with sorrow, but the hiding of my Father's face.

* * * * * * *

I have had but one letter from Alanson, which was written in January. Brother Creesy has written me twice. His letters and yours are all I have received from home.

Love to all who love our Lord.

HARRIET."

Malinda Phelps, the seventh child and third daughter of Eliphalet and Mehitable Phelps, was born in New Marlboro, Mass., October 7th, 1801.

With her parents she came to Ohio and lived there with them until her marriage to Gamaliel Wilcox, on the 18th of April, 1825. The father of Gamaliel Wilcox was one of the very earliest settlers of the township of Wayne, the family being one of sterling character. Uncle Gamaliel lived on a farm only a short distance from where Grandfather Phelps lived, and his farm was very near the old church so often mentioned. When I first went to Ohio I was taken to the house of Uncle Gamaliel, and there I first met any of my father's kindred in Ohio, except having seen my Uncle Alanson at Hudson on the journey there.

I remember Aunt Malinda as a very kind and affectionate woman, who was much beloved by all her relatives. She never had any children, or at least none that lived to any age, if she had any at all.

Grandfather Phelps died in March, 1842, and Aunt Malinda died in December of the same year, so the family had great sorrow that year.

As she lived for some five years after my arrival, and as the families of the two sisters, Malinda and Aurelia, were very intimate, I saw much of her and became very much attached to her. Being so young, however, I cannot now recall very much about her personal appearance.

Dyantha Phelps, the eighth child and fourth daughter of Eliphalet and Mehitable Phelps, was born in New Marlboro, Mass., November 2d, 1804.

She also came with her parents to Ohio, and in February of the year 1825 she was married to Pliny Case, a young man, a native of Connecticut, who had settled in Wayne and taken up a farm almost exactly opposite that of Harvey Walter already alluded to. He had built a log house, and took his wife there after their marriage. They had one daughter, named Julia, but she died when very young. Aunt Dyantha died August 16th, 1828.

In the letter of Aunt Harriet, a part of which has been copied, she refers as follows to her sister Dyantha: "When I asked sister Dyantha 'if she ever felt any concern about little Julia,' she answered: 'O no! she will be taken care of while *you* live, and then there is the same God and the same promises remain.'"

Other than what is here written the editor has no knowledge of his Aunt Dyantha.

Aurelia Phelps, the ninth child of Eliphalet and Mehitable Phelps, was born in New Marlboro, Mass., November 28th, 1804, and died April, 1806.

Aurelia Phelps second, the tenth child and sixth daughter of Eliphalet and Mehitable Phelps was born in New Marlboro, Mass., March 22d, 1806.

So far as known she received what education she had in New Marlboro, and it is supposed that, when her parents went to Ohio, she did not accompany them, but remained in Massachusetts for a few years—possibly to obtain more education, as she was only about 12 years old when they removed to Ohio. After she became a young lady she went to the city of New York and spent about one year in the family of her favorite brother, Asa Hosmer Phelps, after which she went to Ohio, arriving there after the death of her sister Dyantha. She was a favorite sister of her brother Asa Hosmer, and she always cherished for him a warm affection.

She was married to Pliny Case in Wayne, Ohio, on the 19th day of June, 1827.

Their children were:

First. Alexander Case, born in Wayne, April 16th, 1828, died 1828.

Second. Harriet Phelps Case, born in Wayne, January 10th, 1833.

Third. Sylvester Burt Case, born in Wayne, December 14th, 1838, died December 12th, 1839.

Margaret Malinda Case, born in Wayne, March 8th, 1842, died February 28th, 1893.

Fifth. Julia Eliza Case, born in Wayne, March 8th, 1842, died March 10th, 1842.

Sixth. Caturah Case, born in Wayne, December 20th, 1842, died February 3d, 1843.

As the writer was sent by his mother, after the death of his father, to live with and be brought up by his Aunt Aurelia, his information touching her life and surroundings is still vivid in his mind.

Arriving in the fall of the year of 1837, when he was in his sixth year, he found his aunt living in a log house, with the following family around her: In addition to her husband, there was a younger brother of his, a young man named Lauren Case; there was a young girl about 14 or 15 years of age, a daughter of Uncle Harvey Phelps, named Anna Phelps; a boy about 11 or 12 years of age named Maverick Wakeman, and her own daughter, Harriet, then nearly 5 years old. It was a new and at that time a wild and hard country, with none of the appliances or refinements of civilization. The forest trees had only been cleared off in comparatively small areas of land—a few acres in extent around the homes of the different settlers.

There were settlers living at intervals of from one half to one mile from each other throughout the township. All were very poor, and it was hard work to make a living. Money was extremely scarce, and they had to deal with each other and the stores with such products as they could produce on their farms. The lives of both men and women were very hard. Aunt Aurelia was a tall and strong woman when in her prime, and could turn off an immense amount of work of the very hardest kind.

She used to take the wool as it came off the back of the sheep, card, comb, spin, color and weave it into various kinds of cloth for men and women's wear, and then cut and make the garments herself.

She also carded, spun and wove all kinds of linen and tow cloth for men's summer wear, and wove and made table linen and towelling. She was also a very swift person with the knitting needle, knitting great numbers of woolen stockings and mittens for winter wear. She was a kind and obliging neighbor—efficient in sickness, often going at night to assist the sick and dying, and was capable of doing almost everything that required to be done in such trying scenes of life.

She was an extremely conscientious woman in all matters relating to her religious life and belief. Like her sister Harriet already referred to, she had a horror of card-playing and dancing, and was also almost puritanical in her views of keeping the Sabbath day. She lived in Wayne until the spring of 1844, when her husband sold his farm there and removed to the township of Greene, Trumbull county, where she lived on their farm until her death, on the 19th day of February, 1880.

She was a true Christian, fearless in her faith, and when the summons came for her to go up higher, she resigned her soul into the care of her Heavenly Father with perfect trust.

Mary Porter Phelps, the eleventh child and seventh daughter of Eliphalet and Mehitable Phelps, was born in New Marlboro, Mass., November 21st, 1808.

She accompanied her parents to Ohio. On the 8th day of November, 1827, she was married to Linus H. Jones, a young man of excellent family of the town of Wayne. They lived in happiness less than one year, when God called her to a happier and purer life.

Uncle Linus once told the writer that she was a handsome, vivacious and lovely woman. The love of Uncle Linus for the relatives of his youthful wife was often manifested to them in various ways during the long years of his useful and active life. She left no issue.

Ann Eliza Phelps, the fourteenth child and eighth daughter of Eliphalet and Mehitable Phelps, was born in New Marlboro, Mass., December 14th, 1814.

She also went to Ohio with her father and mother, and on the 20th of November, 1834, she was married to Dryden Creesy, of Cherry Valley, Ashtabula county, Ohio. She bore him one son, named Alanson Creesy, but he died when a young lad about 7 or 8 years of age. She died April 30th, 1840. I remember having seen her.

This completes the record of the daughters of Eliphalet and Mehitable Phelps. A curious fact about them is that of the six daughters who married, not one of them left a son to grow to manhood, and only two aunts, Hannah and Aurelia, left daughters who lived to grow to womanhood. They each left two daughters who lived to womanhood.

They were all women of sterling character, and left their impress upon the early civilization of that part of Ohio in which they had their homes.

CHAPTER X.

The Sons of Eliphalet Phelps.

Asahel Phelps, the Seventh Generation.

Asahel Phelps, the second child and first son of Eliphalet and Mehitable Phelps, was born (probably) in New Marlboro, Mass., March 16th, 1791. He married Rhoda Norton in New Marlboro, December 15th, 1817.

She was the daughter of David and Rachel Norton, and was born in New Marlboro, Mass., January 28th, 1785.

Asahel Phelps removed to the town of Wales, Erie county, New York, previous to the year, or very early in the year 1821, and lived on his farm there until his death on March 12th, 1844.

The children of Asahel and Rhoda Phelps were:

First. Julia A. Phelps, born in New Marlboro, April 17th, 1819, died July 10th, 1895.

Second. Martin Phelps, born in Wales Centre, N. Y., March 29th, 1821, and died March 30th, 1860.

Third. Margery M. Phelps, born in Wales Centre, N. Y., March 29th, 1821, and died August, 11th, 1886.

Fourth. David N. Phelps, born in Wales Centre, N. Y., March 9th, 1824.

The writer remembers having seen his Uncle Asahel once in his lifetime, when he came with his wife from his home in Erie county, New York, to visit his relatives in Wayne, Ohio, probably about the year 1840.

Of his character or history I have no data upon which to form an opinion, but I am convinced that they were both good, and that he was a man who stood well in the community in which he lived.

I visited his widow one day in the summer of the year 1847, when a young lad, in company with my mother and my brother, William S. Phelps. I also remember of visiting his grave in the graveyard situated near the family home.

CHAPTER XI.

HARVEY PHELPS, THE SEVENTH GENERATION.

Harvey Phelps, the third child and second son of Eliphalet and Mehitable Phelps, was born in New Marlboro, Mass., August 19th, 1793.

The writer has no data to show at what date he went to Ohio.

It is possible, and perhaps probable, that if Harvey Walter went to Ohio before the family of Grandfather Phelps removed there, that Harvey Phelps accompanied his brother-in-law to that then far western State.

If he went with his father to Ohio he must have been about 25 years old when he arrived there.

He married Betsy Meacham in Gustavus, Trumbull county, Ohio, November 9th, 1820, and he died in Richmond, Ashtabula county, Ohio, August 16th, 1853.

He owned a farm near the center of the town of Williamsfield, Ashtabula county, where he lived a great many years and brought up his family, his farm adjoining that of his younger brother, Reuben Phelps, whose record will appear in due sequence.

The children of Harvey and Betsy Phelps were:

First. Francis D. Phelps, born in Williamsfield, December 21st, 1821, and died June 17th, 1893.

Second. Anna Phelps, born in Williamsfield, January 16th, 1823.

Third. Harriet Phelps, born in Williamsfield, March 21st, 1826.

Fourth. Hannah Phelps, born in Williamsfield, April 17th, 1829, and died May 25th, 1856.

Fifth. Sarah Jane Phelps, born in Williamsfield, February 10th, 1831, and died November 10th, 1872.

Sixth. James Madison Phelps, born in Williamsfield, February 10th, 1833.

Seventh. George Monroe Phelps, born in Williamsfield, February 10th, 1833, and died April 20th, 1861.

Eighth. Mary Phelps, born in Williamsfield, December 10th, 1836, and died November 3d, 1893.

Ninth. Percis Phelps, born in Williamsfield, August 16th, 1838.

Tenth. William Phelps, born in Williamsfield, December 4th, ——, and died August 5th, 1893.

Like some of his sisters, Uncle Harvey was an extremely conscientious man in the manifestation of his religious belief. He and Uncle Reuben loved to attend a Wesleyan Methodist revival meeting, and take part in it, and they could shout "Glory to God" and "Amen" with great fervor and unction. The emotional in religious work was more prevalent then than it is now in these latter days. I remember Uncle Harvey and his family, and of visiting them in my early years.

CHAPTER XII.

ASA HOSMER PHELPS, THE SEVENTH GENERATION.

Asa Hosmer Phelps—the father of the writer—was the fourth child and third son of Eliphalet and Mehitable Phelps, and was born in New Marlboro, Mass., April 20th, 1795.

Of his early life and surroundings we have no definite knowledge; all have faded away in the dim obscurity of the many years that have passed since he died, December 14th, 1835.

He is said to have been a man of about 5 feet 11 inches in height, of dark hair and eyes, a handsome form, and possessing a sweet and melodious voice, was a fine singer. As stated before he was the idol of his sisters. By trade he was a saddle, harness and trunk maker, but where he learned the trade is unknown—probably in Massachusetts.

He made the old-fashioned, round-topped trunks covered with calfskin, tanned with the hair on, and fastened with small, round-headed brass nails, which was the usual method of making trunks in those days.

I remember having seen two or three of the trunks he made when I was a child in Ohio.

ASA HOSMER PHELPS

He never went to Ohio. It is presumed that when the family went to the west, that he emigrated to New York City, or to that vicinity. At what year he went there is now unknown. It is possible that he never lived in New York City until after his marriage to Margery McCoun, in Oyster Bay, Long Island, July 22d, 1819.

She was the youngest child and fifth daughter of William and Sarah (Townsend) McCoun, and was born in Oyster Bay, Long Island, March 10th, 1799. She came of an old and distinguished Long Island family of well-to-do people. For many years before the revolution they had lived near Oyster Bay, on Long Island Sound, and there Asa Hosmer Phelps met her, and there they were married July 22d, 1819.

They first went to live at a little hamlet named Norwich, not far from Oyster Bay, and here their first two children were born.

The following are the children of Asa Hosmer and Margery (McCoun) Phelps:

First. William Sydney Phelps, born in Norwich, L. I., April 17th, 1820.

Second. Emma Aurelia Phelps, born in Norwich, L. I., October 27th, 1821, and died in Brooklyn, N. Y., November 20th, 1889.

Third. Sarah Sophia Phelps, born in Oyster Bay, L. I., February 22d, 1823, and died in Brooklyn, N. Y., April 15th, 1861.

Fourth. Augustus Eliphalet Phelps, born in New York City, May 2d, 1825, and died in

San Francisco, California, October, 15th, 1892.

Fifth. Alanson Hosmer Phelps, born in New York City, February 10th, 1832.

Sixth. Daniel Townsend Phelps, born in New York City, April 21st, 1835.

I have nothing that shows where my parents lived during their early life in New York, but in after years, during the later years of my father's life, they lived in Essex street (in which street the writer was born), and in DeLancy street. He followed the occupation of saddle and harness making, and so far as known, supported his family in comfort.

While residing in New York City he joined the New York Volunteer Fire Department. At that time they had no engines for extinguishing fires, but had to depend upon buckets of water, handing them from man to man to put out fires.

During his attendance at a fire he took a severe cold by getting wet—a cold from which he never recovered. The effects of it were disastrous to him and his family, as it finally terminated in consumption, from which disease he died on the 14th day of December, 1835, in his 41st year, leaving his widow with six young children to battle with the world, and without leaving them any means of a livelihood.

Some years before his death he had sent his eldest son (William) up to Oyster Bay to live with his Uncle Daniel McCoun.

Personally I can remember but very little about my father, as I was only about 3 years and 10 months old when he died, but I do remember seeing him at work in his little shop —of seeing him when he was sick during his last illness, and of coming home in a carriage from the funeral.

Up to his last sickness he had never made any profession of religion, but during his fatal illness he made his peace with God and died in the faith of Jesus Christ. In my possession is a part of a letter written by him on his death bed to his friends in Ohio, but it was not signed by him; this I regret very much, as it would have been a satisfaction to his sons to have had at least *one* of his autographs. Evidently he wrote the letter, and becoming weary he laid it aside, hoping to finish it at some future time, which probably he never was able to do.

When read between the lines, especially the latter part of it shows, to my mind, a man of noble character, void of pretense or hypocrisy, and bears internal evidence of deep thoughtfulness, and as if actuated by high principle. It is copied here for three reasons: First, that it may be preserved; second, to show the condition, character and feelings of the man at that critical period of his life; and, third, becanse it is the only specimen of his composition extant, and therefore contains the only authentic language or words known to have been used by him.

The letter is as follows, although some few

corrections have been made in spelling, punctuation, etc:

"NEW YORK, Monday, Nov. 23d, 1835.
My Dear Parents, Brothers and Sisters:

I take this opportunity to write to you all in this letter, as it is probable the last that I shall be ever able to write you again.

I commenced on the 19th to write to Aurelia, but Marga had wrote to Harriet some time since. We expected an answer, but your letter never came to hand. I then felt miserable bad, but since I have found that my disease, which has been of the liver complaint, which has thrown me into the hasty consumption and consumed all of my flesh and strength, and left me just able to walk from the bed to the fire. The probability is that ere the moon wanes twice more I shall be gone from this land of pain and sorrow. I was taken on Monday, the second week in September, with a violent cough, which lasted me six or seven weeks; was constant day and night until I got so far exhausted that nature gave way. I got some sleep, and then I commenced to take laudanum to relieve my pain, which it did. I then called in our family doctor, who ordered me to take blood root, which I found to leave me in either a feverish state, or with a dry cough.

In the meantime I had chills every day but no fever until midnight, and then I have seen some curious and singular scenes, but not interesting at the present time, but at some other would be worth noticing.

I then found that my complaint was becoming seated in my left side.

The dry and hacking cough which had so long kept me in such misery—for such was my distress—that I could not sleep for twenty-four hours.

I then concluded that my fate was sealed, and when I called the doctor he recommended a blister to be drawn on any part of the chest, and that it be kept running as long as it well could be by applying a salve for dressing it that would draw it sufficient to keep it open.

It seemed then that this blister, or some island moss which I had recommended to me by some of my neighbors, had given me relief from that dry, hacking cough, and from that time I have had no difficulty in raising the matter that gathered in my breast and side. If you recollect I was sick for months with a very bad cough, and that lasted me until warm weather in the spring, but when the warm weather set in the cough left me from May to September, but now it is progressing in the way above stated. I have wanted to see some one of my friends, if no more, but I fear that I shall never do on this side of the great gulf supposed to be existing between God and man. What then does this great space contain?

Does it contain the numerous spirits, the dead bodies that have gone before us? I presume it does, but my weak mind cannot fathom this.

But then look around you! Look at all the different denominations who term themselves Christians! Where will you find any one from the highest to the lowest but what is looking for self, and his selfish societies. I cast no reflections upon any one, but I speak free and independent of all, and think as each and every one must think who has looked over these scenes with an impartial eye. But of these scenes I know I have said enough, for I know that they are so far from your belief.

Here I will try to give a short sketch of my past life. When I left home I left at an age when the youthful mind hardly becomes stable enough to think of these things. I mixed in early life with various sects of religious denominations, and was always fond of going to meeting. For many years after I left home, as I became more acquainted in different societies, I used to go less to church, and have not been a very regular attendant since. After I came to New York I attended almost all of the different denominations, and what did I see? I saw from the highest to the lowest all striving to gain their point by all the intrigue that laid in their power to draw the weak minds of their fellow creatures over to their selfish purposes; then it was that I thought if this is religion it is no religion for me.

From that time, which is ten or twelve years since, I have left them all from that time to this. What will be the sequel God only knows.

I have had the advice and prayers of a loving wife for years, who, no doubt, has felt for me all those ties of love and affection which nature gives and the Christian heart could feel."

Here ends his letter. Attached to the same sheet is the following in the handwriting of his wife: "He said, speaking of the letter, 'My mind is altogether changed, but wish to send it just as it is to let my parents see the difference in my views. I feel now that I am a sinner saved by grace; before I was trusting in my own good works to save me, but now I feel I have none, that Jesus Christ is my Saviour; I desire no other; he is just such a Saviour as I need.' Yours in love,

M. PHELPS."

There were then no methods of taking pictures of faces as we have now, as that was long before the discovery of the photographic art, and yet I have in my possession a silhouette of my father's face done in black. The picture originally belonged to Aunt Harriet; after her death it fell by inheritance to Aunt Aurelia, and during my visit to Ohio in 1881, three years after the death of the latter, her daughter Harriet gave it to me. It shows a good face, or profile, although it cannot show the expression of his features. What his general character was other than what has already been written we know but little, but reasoning from analogy, and bearing in mind the general characteristics of his parents, of his brothers and sisters, what good men and women they all were, it is certainly reasonable to *infer* that he was a good man and a good citizen. A *poor* man we know he was, but as that has been the fate of some of the best men the world has produced, we need not feel that that was any stain or disgrace upon his name.

That Asa Hosmer Phelps and Margery McCoun were a very *handsome couple* when they were married we are very sure was true. From the traditions that have come down about him regarding his good looks, and from the appearance of our mother in middle life, and in her old age, we may believe that she was a fine-looking and stylish girl. They were married in 1819, and as he died in 1835, their married life lasted only a little over sixteen years. In that time they had six children.

For the preservation of the record of the family I copy here the names of Grandfather and Grandmother McCoun, and the names of their children, with the date of birth and the death of each so far as the records show:

William McCoun, born August 28th, 1750, died March 3d, 1818.

Sarah (Townsend) McCoun, born --, ——, died February 11th, 1825.

Their children were:

First. Hannah McCoun, born September 16th, 1781, died February 13th, 1815.

Second. Phœbe McCoun, born June 6th, 1784, died April 20th, 1820.

Third. William Townsend McCoun, born August 8th, 1786, died July 18th, 1878.

Fourth. Abigail McCoun, born March 1st, 1789, died November 16th, 1861.

Fifth. Susannah McCoun, born June 9th, 1791, died February —, 1830.

Sixth. Daniel McCoun, born November 28th, 1793, died October 20th, 1875.

Seventh. Sydney McCoun, born September 8th, 1796, died September 25th, 1813.

Eighth. Margery McCoun, born March 10th, 1799, died November 16th, 1884.

Of these brothers and sisters of Margery McCoun Phelps, the writer knows but very little of any of them, with the exception of his Uncle Townsend, his Aunt Abigail, and his Uncle Daniel. These three I remember having seen, but none of the others. Uncle Townsend McCoun was a distinguished lawyer of great ability, and amassed quite a fortune at his practice at the bar, and was at one time the Vice-Chancellor of the State of New York.

Mother was a *business* woman. She knew how to make money, and as quite as desirable a qualification she generally knew how to keep it.

After the death of her husband she did not sit down and repine at her fate, thinking that the sun had set for good, or that God had turned His face away from her, but with noble resolution and courage she commenced at once to do something to support her family.

Uncle Townsend was kind to her, and helped her in various ways.

As already stated, her eldest son, William, had been sent away from home to live with his Uncle Daniel some years before the death of his father. She arranged to have the second son, Augustus, then about 10 years of age, sent to Oyster Bay to live with an old friend of her family, Mr. Henry Fleet.

At the time of which I am now writing *beads* of various sizes, colors and styles were much affected by the devotees of fashion.

There were several large firms in New York

then engaged in importing large quantities of these goods from Italy and France.

They came in all sizes—from the tiniest sizes as small as the heads of the smallest pins, to sizes at least a quarter of an inch in diameter. They were used by fashionable ladies for working into bags and reticules. They were also exported to Mexico, and also went to the Indian traders of the far west to sell to Indians for furs.

They came from Europe strung on *grass*, and as they were often badly broken and mixed together, it was necessary to have them assorted and re-strung on silk or linen thread.

Mother, with the assistance of some friends, made the acquaintance of two or three large dealers in these goods, and made an agreement with them to assort and re-string the beads for them.

This was work that little girls could do, and having two little girls of her own who were then old enough to assist her, she went to work at once, and within a comparatively short time she had conquered the difficulties of the business, and had quite a good paying business in a small way. Before many months she had a good many other girls and women at work—sometimes having from thirty to forty on her pay roll.

She continued the business for several years—just how many is now unknown—but I think she followed it until her own daughters became of a marriageable age. She was living at this time at No. 165 DeLancy street, New

York, and continued to live in the same house for some years after the marriage of her eldest daughter. Her sister, Abigail McCoun, then lived with her. Augustus was also living with her at the time, or rather after he came back from Mr. Fleet's. He came to New York to learn the bookbinding trade with Harper & Brothers, and while learning his trade he lived at home with his mother. After the marriage of her youngest daughter to Mr. Isaac Hall, which was in 1842, she discontinued keeping house, and went to live with Mr. and Mrs. Hall.

A few years after the death of her daughter, Mrs. Hall, which occurred in 1861, and after the emigration of all of her sons to California, she came to the latter State in the year 1863, and from that date to the time of her death in 1884, she made California her permanent home, living nearly all the time with her son, Augustus E. Phelps.

She died in his house November 16th, 1884, holding her mental faculties to the last, and was buried in Laurel Hill Cemetery, in San Francisco.

CHAPTER XIII.

REUBEN PHELPS, THE SEVENTH GENERATION.

Reuben Phelps, the fifth child and fourth son of Eliphalet and Mehitable Phelps, was born in New Marlboro, Mass., February 27th, 1797.

His eldest son states that he came to Ohio two or three years before his father came. The writer is firmly of the opinion that both Harvey and Reuben Phelps, and probably Harvey Walter and his wife, Hannah Phelps, came to Ohio all together as early as 1816, and possibly in 1815.

If they came as early as 1815 Reuben was then a very young man to start out into a new country, as he would then have been only 18 years old. He settled on a farm on the east side of the road, a short distance north of the center of the town of Williamsfield, Ashtabula county, a farm adjoining that of his brother Harvey, where he lived all his life, and where he died in his old homestead on March 3d, 1860.

He married Olive Leonard in Williamsfield, February 4th, 1818.

She was the daughter of Levi Leonard and Kezia (Benjamin) Leonard, and was born in Massachusetts, November 29th, 1801.

Their children were:

First. James H. Phelps, born in Williamsfield, December 14th, 1819.

Second. Dyantha Phelps, born in Williamsfield, March 12th, 1825, and died September 5th, 1841.

Third. Mary P. Phelps, born in Williamsfield, November 7th, 1828, and died October 25th, 1889.

Fourth. Aurelia Phelps, born in Williamsfield, November 13th, 1838.

Fifth. Joseph B. Phelps, born in Williamsfield, July 26th, 1840.

Sixth. Reuben Phelps, Jr., born in Williamsfield, November 3d, 1841, and died August 2d, 1869.

Seventh. Lemuel B. Phelps, born in Williamsfield, September 18th, 1843, and died June 30th, 1887.

Reuben Phelps was a man of about 5 feet 6 or 7 inches in height, and of dark complexion. He was an ardent and enthusiastic Christian, always ready to give a reason for the hope he cherished of an immortal life beyond the grave. His greatest happiness seemed to be to attend the numerous Methodist or Wesleyan revival meetings that in his time were frequently held in the vicinity.

He was a good singer, and was capable of taking part in such meetings, either by leading the singing, speaking, or leading in extemporaneous prayer.

He sleeps in the old burying ground located just across the road from his home in Williamsfield.

Alanson Woodward Phelps, the twelfth child and fifth son of Eliphalet and Mehitable Phelps, was born in New Marlboro, Mass., June —, 1810, and died October 10th, 1810.

REVEREND ALANSON PHELPS

CHAPTER XIV.

ALANSON PHELPS, THE SEVENTH GENERATION.

Alanson Phelps, the thirteenth child and sixth son of Eliphalet and Mehitable Phelps was born in New Marlboro, Mass., February 10th, 1812.

If Eliphalet Phelps and his family went to Ohio from Massachusetts in 1818, as referred to in Chapter VIII, the subject of this sketch was in his seventh year when he arrived in Ohio, and he must have seen in his childish way the struggles of his parents to make a living in that then new and undeveloped country. That the facilities for obtaining an education were then very limited, there is no doubt, and where he first attended school in Ohio is now unknown. When he became a man, through the assistance of his sister, Harriet Phelps, he was enabled to take a course of instruction in the Western Reserve College at Hudson, Ohio, where he graduated from college either in 1839 or 1840. He was the only member of the family of Eliphalet Phelps that had the good fortune to obtain a collegiate education. The writer believes that it was also through the good influence of his sister Harriet that he was induced to enter the Christian ministry.

The following account of his life has been written by his fourth daughter, Mrs. Louisa Kimball (Phelps) Wyman, for this book:

"In his early manhood he graduated at the Western Reserve College, then located at Hudson, Summit county, Ohio, after which he went to the Theological Seminary of the Protestant Episcopal Church in Alexandria, Va., where he graduated and was ordained to the diaconate, July 18th, 1841, by Bishop Moore of Virginia. He returned to Ohio directly after his ordination, and was married August 31st of the same year to Miss Mary Ann Bronson, then residing at Peninsula, Summit county, Ohio.

"She was the only surviving daughter of Rev. Abraham and Sabra (Way) Bronson, and was born in Arlington, Vt., November 7th, 1814.

"Their children were:

"First. Emma Lydia Phelps, born in Peninsula, Ohio, July 28th, 1842.

"Second. Ann Eliza Phelps, born in Hudson, Ohio, March 10th, 1843, and died November 12th, 1862.

"Third. Mary Bronson Phelps, born in Hudson, Ohio, November 8th, 1845.

"Fourth. Louisa Kimball Phelps, born in Hudson, Ohio, September 2d, 1847.

"Alanson Phelps was ordained to the priesthood in 1842, by Bishop McIlwain, in Ross Chapel, in Gambier, Ohio.

"During his ministry he had charge of

parishes as follows: In Hudson, Ohio, from 1842 to 1849; in Franklin Mills (now Kent), Ohio, from 1849 to 1854; in Painesville, Lake County, Ohio, from 1854 to 1860, and in Fremont, Ohio, from 1860 to 1865. His ministry was successful, and the parishes under his efficient care increased in numbers and influence.

"For many years he labored under great bodily infirmity, which finally so overcame him that he was obliged to give up active ministerial work, and after resigning the charge of the parish at Fremont, he removed again to Painesville, which was his home, until his death, which occurred in Painesville on November 5th, 1889.

"Mrs. Mary Ann (Bronson) Phelps died in Painesville, November 28th, 1857.

"On the 29th of September, 1859, Rev. Alanson Phelps was married in Christ Church, Hartford, Conn., to Miss Jane Eliza Ensworth, daughter of John and Eliza (Bunce) Ensworth. She was born in Andover, Conn., April 21st, 1820. They had no children. She survived him but one year, dying in Manchester, Vt., October 8th, 1890."

The following account of his life has been furnished the editor by his third daughter, Miss Mary Bronson Phelps:

"Rev. Alanson Phelps was specially interested in the cause of public education, and whatever tended to promote its growth. His life in Virginia, during his seminary days, interested him in the colored race, and he espoused the cause of the negro, although contrary to the spirit of the times. Many of these he taught to read and write, and he gave his service freely when he could do them good.

"Later in life he took an active interest in common schools, and aimed as far as possible to develop a literary spirit in the community where he lived. His help was freely given in sustaining literary societies, and he delivered many lectures on different subjects of science and other matters suited to the times.

"Becoming convinced of the advantage of belonging to some one of the various orders or societies popular at the time, he joined the Order of Free and Accepted Masons, and was an enthusiastic member of Knights Templar, retaining his interest to the end of his life.

"After the failure of his health, and his consequent retirement from the active work of the ministry, he sought recreation in travel, and accompanied by his wife he made several trips to California, where he was ever a great admirer of its climate, its scenery and the hospitality of its people. He visited all parts of the State, and the many enthusiastic letters written for the various periodicals of his home in Ohio, testified to his enjoyment of that wonderful country.

"In 1872 he, with his wife, made the tour of Europe, where they spent many months traveling through the Old World, and from that time he traveled so extensively that at the time of his death there were few places of interest in this country or Europe which he had not visited. His travels, as well as his position, brought him in contact with many distinguished people, and he numbered among his friends many men prominent in State and Church.

"The years of his age were more than three score and ten, and when he departed this life suddenly in his 78th year, it was like a sheaf of wheat fully ripe for the sickle, but rich in the fulfillment of the harvest, and 'meet for the Master's use.'"

Rev. Alanson Phelps was a man spare in form, and when in his prime stood very erect in figure, of distinguished appearance, a man of remarkable dignity of bearing, in height about 6 feet 1 inch, and with coal black hair and piercing black eyes.

His manners were ever quiet and somewhat reserved, and his conversation was modulated to a low tone of voice.

He was, however, a genial and cordial companion to all his friends and acquaintances, and was universally liked by his neighbors.

In the early manhood of the editor of this work he had the happiness to spend nearly or quite a year in the family of this uncle.

During that period of time he, the editor, passed through a very severe siege of illness, and at that time of pain and sorrow this uncle cared for him with the tenderness of a father towards a beloved son. In point of fact he was more like a father to the writer than any other he has ever known. Having been named after him, there was a bond of affection between the two which was never sundered so long as the uncle lived. He was a man chary of giving advice, but his conduct and deportment were complete in moral excellence, and his life was the perfect bloom of a Christian gentleman's character.

He was not a florid or a very ornate speaker, but as a sermonizer he compared favorably with the other rectors of the Episcopal Church in Ohio, as it existed in his day, his sermons being calculated to inspire to higher and purer motives of conduct in his hearers.

By the death of his first wife, who had been an invalid for several years, suffering from the dreadful disease of consumption, he was left with four young daughters to struggle with the world, and for whom at that time there was need of a firm hand and a kind woman's heart to lead them on in life. By his second marriage he won a lady of surpassing loveliness of disposition, and who, coming into his family, became the very ideal of a loving mother to the four motherless girls whom she found awaiting her when he brought her to his home after their bridal trip.

She took them at once to her heart, and she became to them all a mother indeed. Rev. Mr. Phelps and his wife were among the first tourists to come to California over the newly-constructed railroads—the Union and Central Pacific—

arriving here immediately after the completion of these roads in the early summer of 1869. This was his first visit to the State. Here he met for the first time some of his nephews, the sons of his brother Asa Hosmer Phelps. He was the only paternal uncle all of these nephews had ever known. His coming seemed like a benediction to them, and each time when he went away, they parted from him and his lovable wife with great regret. He made four visits in all to the State, the last visit in 1885, leaving the State in the spring of 1886.

He was always happy while in California, and having no sons of his own, his heart seemed to go out to these nephews as if they were his own children.

He was a devout and consistent churchman, holding the orthodox faith as taught by the thirty-nine articles of the Episcopal Church.

He was not obtrusive in his religious life—he never wore his religion on his sleeve for "daws to peck at," but as a calm, consistent, Christian gentleman. It affords the writer great pleasure to pen these few lines in affectionate remembrance of the beautiful character of the Reverend Alanson Phelps. His influence was felt for good wherever he made his home.

He sleeps the sleep of the just in the family lot in Oakwood Cemetery, Fremont, Ohio, where the remains of his two wives, and his daughter, rest in peace.

CHAPTER XV.

THE FAMILY OF ASA HOSMER PHELPS.

WILLIAM SYDNEY PHELPS, THE EIGHTH GENERATION.

William Sydney Phelps, the first child of Asa Hosmer and Margery (McCoun) Phelps was born at Norwich, near Oyster Bay, Long Island, April 17th, 1820. His early life was passed on Long Island, living there with his parents until they removed to the city of New York, which occurred within a few years after his birth. As heretofore stated, when he was about 8 years of age his parents sent him to live with his maternal uncle, Daniel McCoun, at Oyster Bay, where he was occupied as boys usually are on and around a farm. Here he attended a private school for a very few weeks. Daniel McCoun being a blacksmith as well as a farmer, William in time began to assist his uncle with his blacksmithing, and by this means he acquired a knowledge of that trade.

He lived with his uncle in Oyster Bay until the latter removed to the city of Brooklyn, about the year 1833, where he bought out and carried on a horseshoeing establishment. William accompanied him to Brooklyn. While there he

WILLIAM SYDNEY PHELPS

used to wander with other boys around what are now Brooklyn Heights, where at that time were many orchards of apple trees growing, the fruit of which the boys helped themselves to as often as they could get a chance.

Daniel McCoun only remained in Brooklyn about two or three years, and then returned to Oyster Bay, taking William with him.

About the year 1839, when William was 19 years of age, Daniel McCoun removed his family from Long Island to South Wales, Erie county, New York, taking William with him. Here Mr. McCoun entered upon the clearing off of a new farm, the building of a saw-mill, and various other enterprises in which William took an active part. He lived here with his uncle until he became a man. On the 10th of October, 1844, he was married to Miss Minerva McCall, the only daughter of Ira and Selecia (Seely) McCall. She was born in South Wales, Erie county, New York, February 2d, 1823.

She was a woman of an amiable and lovely disposition, and possessed the charms of heart and mind to make a happy home.

Their children were:

First. Emma Margery Phelps, born in Aurora, Erie county, New York, August 16th, 1846, and died in San Francisco, Cal., March 3d, 1862.

Second. Daniel Sydney Phelps, born in

Brooklyn, N. Y., January 23d, 1848, and died July 6th, 1848.

Third. Charles Ira Phelps, born in Brooklyn, February 2d, 1852.

Fourth. William Phelps, born in Brooklyn, February 2d, 1852, died February, 3d, 1852.

Fifth. Augustus Phelps, born in Brooklyn, February 2d, 1852, died February 3d, 1852.

Minerva (McCall) Phelps died in Brooklyn, N. Y., February 9th, 1852, and with her little children sleeps in Greenwood Cemetery, Brooklyn.

After his marriage William was engaged in several occupations—sometimes in blacksmithing, but during the latter years of his residence in South Wales was engaged in the flour-milling business.

In the summer of 1847 his mother, Margery Phelps, went on a visit to South Wales to see her brother, and when she returned to New York in August of 1847, William accompanied her, but without his family, leaving them with his father-in-law, Mr. McCall.

Soon after his arrival in New York he formed a co-partnership with his brother-in-law, Isaac Hall, and they commenced the business of ship-smithing together in the city of New York. After a few months he sent to South Wales for his family, and they immediately went on to New York, where he then commenced housekeeping in the upper part of the house then occupied by Isaac Hall, in Bergen street, Brooklyn. Here he joined the Volunteer Fire Department of the city of Brooklyn, and did his duty as a fireman for a number of years. He was destined, however, to enjoy only about four years of a happy married life in Brooklyn, when death came and called his beloved wife, and he was left alone with two young children to care and provide for.

A short time previous to the death of his wife, his younger brother, Augustus, had returned from California, and after her death the latter persuaded him to go to California.

William sent his two little children to South Wales to be cared for by their maternal grandparents, Mr. and Mrs. Ira McCall, and on the 21st day of May, 1852, they sailed by the steamer "Crescent City," via. the Isthmus of Panama, for California. They crossed the Isthmus by rail twelve miles, thence by boat up the Chagres River to Gorgona, where they took a mule train for Panama. In the Bay of Panama they embarked on the steamer "Northerner," and arrived in San Francisco on the 22d of June, 1852.

Very soon afterwards William secured a lot on Drumm street, San Francisco, near Market street, upon which to build a shop, and formed a co-partnership with a man by the name of Joseph Fick to do a ship-smithing business under the name of Fick & Phelps. They were successful, as there was a great deal of shipping in San Francisco. Prices for their work were high, and they entered upon an era of great prosperity.

After one or two years with Mr. Fick the latter sold out his interest to William, and he then took his brother into partnership with him, under the name of William S. Phelps & Co., and for many years they were the leading firm in that line of mechanism in San Francisco, and the business was successfully carried on by them together, on the original lot where it was first started, until death took Augustus away on the 15th of October, 1892. In the year 1853 they purchased a building lot on the southwest corner of Pacific and Jones streets, San Francisco, where they made their home under the care of a housekeeper. Upon this lot the two brothers always lived side by side. Early in the spring of 1856 William returned to New York by the Isthmus route, and on the 15th day of April, 1856, he was married in Brooklyn to Miss Jane McEwen.

She was the daughter of Peter and Susan (Warren) McEwen, and was born in Unionville, Albany county, New York, August 17th, 1830.

A few days after their marriage they sailed for California by the Isthmus of Panama, accompanied by the two children of William by his first wife. The train by which they crossed the Isthmus was wrecked a few miles from Aspinwall, and out of 1200 passengers on board nearly 250 were killed and wounded, but a kind Providence overshadowed and protected them, and none of the family were injured.

At Panama they went on board the steamer "Golden Age," and arrived in San Francisco upon a very notable day in the history of the city—the 22d day of May, 1856, the day that Casey and Cora were hung by the Vigilance Committee in the presence of 20,000 people. There was intense excitement. William took his family to his house, and they commenced housekeeping at once.

The children of William S. and Jane (McEwen) Phelps were:

First. William Hall Phelps, born in San Francisco, April 17th, 1857.

Second. Minnie Margery Phelps, born in San Francisco, February 19th, 1860.

Third. George Townsend Phelps, born in San Francisco, June 21st, 1862.

Fourth. John Reed Phelps, born in San Francisco, June 21st, 1862.

Fifth. Edwin Corliss Phelps, born in San Francisco, May 22d, 1871.

In December, 1853, William Sydney Phelps took the first degree of Masonry in Golden Gate Lodge of Free and Accepted Masons. In process of time he was elected Junior Deacon, Junior Warden, Senior Warden, and then elected to the office of Worshipful Master of the lodge, which office he held for two years. By virtue of having held the office of Worshipful Master he became eligible as a member of the Grand Lodge of the State of California, and has acted in that capacity for the last twenty-five or more years.

The first sorrow and affliction that came to him in California overtook him by the very sudden death of his beloved daughter, Emma Margery, who sickened and died after an illness of only four days, on the 3d day of March, 1862. She was an interesting and beautiful girl, just budding into womanhood, and gave great promise of maturing into a delightful member of his family, when Death came with his Chariot and bore her away from the pains and sorrows of earth to a fairer and better land.

In the year 1868 William Sydney Phelps was nominated and elected by the Peoples' Party of San Francisco as Supervisor of the Fourth Ward of the city. During his incumbency of that office the paid fire department of the city was organized and put into service, and to this work he devoted a great deal of thought and attention, and saw it successfully inaugurated. He served the city in an honorable and faithful manner for two years, and retired from the office at the end of his term with the good will and esteem of all the good people of the city, as no man could point to him and say that he ever prostituted his office for personal gain. Since his retirement from office at that time he has never sought office again, although he was nominated as a member of the Assembly of the State Legislature but failed of an election.

In writing this epitome of the life of William Sydney Phelps it is almost unavoidable not to give at this place some account of his brother, Augustus Eliphalet Phelps, although a full account of the latter will appear in Chapter XVIII of this book. The two brothers were for many years inseparable as partners, affectionate as brothers, living side by side for thirty-nine years on their property on Pacific and Jones streets, and bringing up their families together in intimate friendship.

As the years went on, Pacific street, on which their houses fronted, became less and less desirable as a street on which to live, and the brothers having considerable frontage of property on Jones street, which was much more desirable as a residence street than Pacific street they decided in the year 1880 to change the location of their houses.

Accordingly early in the summer of that year Augustus had his house raised up, partially turned around, and then removed to the lot owned by him on the west side of Jones street. Immediately following this, William built a large and commodious house adjoining that of his brother on the north side of the latter, furnishing and moving into it in the autumn of 1880. Here they had their homes until death called the younger brother in 1892.

In the year 1868 William S., Augustus E., and Alanson H. Phelps formed a co-partnership under the firm name of Phelps Brothers for the manufacture of bridge and machine bolts, for the manufacture of iron work for bridges and cars, and for doing heavy forging, and the business was continued under that firm name until the year 1873, when it was incorporated under the name of the Phelps Manufacturing Company.

They carried on the business in the same building with that of William S. Phelps & Co. until the year 1882, when they removed the business of the manufacturing company to a tract of land composed of nine fifty vara lots which they had purchased in the previous year, situated on Beach street, west of Black Point, in San Francisco.

Here they met with fair success during the first six or seven years they occupied the property, but after about 1888 the general decline in the iron business began, and during the following years, up to the fall of 1894, they found it impossible to make any money, and in the month of October of that year they had to suspend work, on account of the hard times and the falling off in business.

But amid all the misfortunes of the hard times William Sydney Phelps has ever maintained his integrity as an honest man.

He is a man who has a great many warm and personal friends, some of them of forty years or more acquaintance, and he is going down towards the evening of life with their respect and regard.

EMMA AURELIA PHELPS
(MRS. JOHN M. GRIFFITHS)

CHAPTER XVI.

EMMA AURELIA PHELPS, THE EIGHTH GENERATION.

Emma Aurelia Phelps, the second child and first daughter of Asa Hosmer and Margery (McCoun) Phelps, was born at Norwich, Long Island, October 27th, 1821. Her parents soon afterwards removed to the city of New York, and there she received what education she had, and was brought up in the city. She was a girl of a trim and handsome figure, with light brown hair and blue eyes, very social by nature, and with a soul full of mirth and lightheartedness. She possessed an innate sense of the ludicrous side of life, and had a fine appreciation of all the humorous scenes of city life as they passed before her eyes.

She was a loving daughter, and an able assistant to her mother in her widowhood.

Being such a lovely girl she had many admirers, and among others who came in her train was a young and stylish druggist named John Morton Griffiths, who laid siege to her heart, and finally won it.

He was the third son of William Betts Griffiths (a lieutenant in the American army in the war of 1812-14) and Elizabeth (Cowenhover) Griffiths, and grandson of Lieutenant John Griffifths of the military school of Paris, who came to America with LaFayette to assist the colonists against the British in the war of the revolution, and served in the American army to the end of the war.

Later Lieutenant John Griffiths married Miss Julia Betts of New York, a sister of William Betts, whose farm was located between East Fifty-ninth street and Harlem, and whose farm house was on the old "Cator Road," which ran eastward from the old Boston road towards the East River, not far above Fortieth street.

John Morton Griffiths and Emma Aurelia Phelps were married at the home of her mother in New York City on April 27th, 1841.

Their children were:

First. William Edward Griffiths, born in New York, February 7th, 1842.

Second. Henry Clay Griffiths, born in New York, December 2d, 1844, died February 3d, 1862.

Third. John Morton Griffiths, born in New York, September 13th, 1851.

Dr. John Morton Griffiths was an able chemist and druggist, and opened a drug store at the corner of Grand and Norfolk streets, New York, where he carried on that business for a great many years with considerable success. He was a man of courtly manners, very fastidious in his style of dressing, as he thought every professional man should be.

He brought up two of his sons to be druggists—the eldest and youngest—the second son dying when he was about 17 years of age.

When Mrs. Griffiths was about 33 years of age, she had an attack of inflammatory rheumatism, which left her with an infirmity that remained with her all her life. During the winter of 1857–58 the editor spent several weeks in the family of his sister, and he will never forget her gentle and patient daily life. She was a true and faithful wife to her husband, a warm-hearted and affectionate mother to her sons, and was always ready to help them in any way that would insure their happiness. In the year 1868 her mother made her second visit to California, and in the following year the brothers of Mrs. Griffiths wrote to her inviting her to come to California and make them a visit.

This she did, arriving here in the autumn of 1869, and remained in San Francisco visiting among her four brothers for one year.

This year was one of great happiness to her, and was of equal happiness to her brothers, as she was an agreeable companion, and her presence in the family gatherings was always enjoyed by them.

In the fall of 1870 she returned to New York with her mother, and a few months after her return she removed to Brooklyn.

Her eldest son, Dr. William E. Griffiths,

who had studied medicine, and graduated at the College of Physicians and Surgeons in New York in 1868, and subsequently spent a year in Germany at special studies, decided on his return to establish himself in Brooklyn, and to that city the family removed in 1871, and there his mother made her home to the close of her life.

Owing to the inroads of the rheumatism upon her system, to which reference has been made, during the last twelve or fifteen years of her life she was able to move around but little, and had to remain in her room from month to month and from year to year, without often going down stairs. She bore all these afflictions with the patience of a saint—never complaining or wondering why she had this trial to bear, being satisfied that the Divine Father knew what was best for her. After a few years Dr. Griffiths built for himself a new residence on Schermerhorn street, on the corner of Nevins, in Brooklyn, and in planning the house he designed a large, airy, and spacious room overlooking the street, for his mother, and here, seated in her large arm-chair she spent many happy years. In looking out of her window to see the constant kaleidoscope of city life and fashion pass before her eyes, she had the happy faculty to discern the humorous side of it all. Hers was such a sunny nature that she was able, by herself, to extract amusement and delight from scenes which ordinary people observe but casually.

She was a kind-hearted woman, always ready to do good to others to the extent of her means and strength. She ever cherished a warm affection for her four brothers in California, and when letters came from year to year telling of their success in life, she always rejoiced to hear of their prosperity. She was a noble woman, doing her duty in life, bearing all disappointments with sincere faith and an uncomplaining mind. The rheumatism, from which she suffered in early life, left her with her hands and fingers very much distorted, yet during the long years she occupied her room she was never idle—when she was able to be up—always at work doing some kind of worsted or other fancy work for her friends. She became very expert in the making of "darned net" work, producing numerous pillow-shams and bed-spreads of intricate designs and most remarkable beauty.

These she presented to her friends. Some of these specimens of her work are marvels of beauty, and exhibit a wonderful amount of patience and skill in their construction.

Dr. William Edward Griffiths has furnished the editor with the following tribute, which he has written in affectionate remembrance of his mother:

"Emma Aurelia (Phelps) Griffiths, born in 1821, married in 1841, entered into rest in 1889.

"She had three sons, and being herself possessed of an amiable and patient disposition, as well as excellent judgment, her chief ambition was to insure to her children a good education, and to that end her early instruction fostered the idea of the necessity of learning, and inspired her children with an ambition akin to her own.

"In the midst of her chosen work, and while still a young woman (but 33 years of age), she was afflicted with rheumatism, the result of which, after more than a year of acute suffering, was to cripple her hands and feet to a great degree, and condemn her to a life of invalidism. For all that, her patience and cheerfulness were unconquerable, and under stress of physical pain, the work of benevolence and love which went forth from her sick room, brought comfort and peace to many a sorrowing heart.

"How often were her sympathies enlisted in behalf of the sick and suffering poor, at the recital of my experiences among them professionally, and how often her charitable instincts found a ready and practical means of relief!

"With an ardent love of nature, her interest extended from the simplest fern or wild flower to the terrific manifestations of the thunder storm.

"Music was her delight, and with her sweet and pleasant tones we could always tell her moods by her singing. Now 'Thy Will Be Done,' or 'Praise God From Whom All Blessing Flow,' and again 'My Country 'Tis of Thee,' or 'Home, Sweet Home.'

"There was no room in her heart for injustice, shams, or hypocrisy.

"She entertained a sturdy and steadfast opposition to slavery, and had an abiding faith in its ultimate destruction. Her patriotism was shown by her efforts in behalf of the nation's defenders, and, in making with her poor, lame fingers, the flag, 'the stars and stripes,' which was to float over our home till the war was over, and long past.

"I can almost hear her now: 'Be just and fear not; let all the ends thou aimst at be thy Country's, thy God's, and truth's.'

"Such an one was my mother, and, as such, when the summons came to lay down the burdens of this earthly sojourn, notwithstanding the bodily pain which tortured her at times, her voice, though weak, sang hymns of praise, and her last words were a benediction on her children."

Outside of the revelation of the Bible regarding the immortality of the soul, there are other indisputable evidences of the certainty of a life beyond the grave. One great and wonderful proof of this is that all races of men, in all ages, in a greater or less degree, have believed in a future existence. Infidels may scoff and skeptics may sneer, yet all history proves this truth. It *is* a truth invincible in the human heart, planted there by the great Creator himself, and no infidel with his subtlest sophistry will ever be able to eradicate this belief from the minds of men.

Another proof of the certainty of a future life in a happier world is often afforded by the visions of the dying, when the Saviour of men, or an angel chosen by Him, for an instant holds the gates of heaven ajar for those who are pure in heart to glance within, and to see with their earthly eyes the unspeakable glory of heaven, ere they pass away from earth.

Traditions have come down to the writer of such visions having been vouchsafed to members of our family, ere death clutched them away from this mortal life. Such a manifestation of divine love and favor was given to the subject of this sketch ere death closed her eyes.

From letters received by the editor from the son and a nephew of Mrs. Griffiths, soon after her decease, which occurred on the 20th of November, 1889, he has gleaned the following. Her nephew wrote:

"Aunt Emma has been an invalid for thirty-five years; seven years before my blessed mother's death she was taken sick, and very nearly all that time she has been confined to her room, her life a benediction of peace and love to all who visited her. Always cheerful, uncomplaining, ready to laugh with those who were merry, or to weep with those who wept.

"What was the secret? *She* knew the source of happiness.

"Although undemonstrative over her religious convictions, yet constantly she was in communication with her God at the throne of grace.

"Several weeks ago she was taken quite sick, so that she had to take to her bed much against her will. It was to be her last sickness.

"She knew that the summons had come for her to set her house in order, and to be ready when the Bridegroom came. I have no doubt in my own mind that this communication, or vision, which came so vividly to her then was only a foretaste of what she would soon enjoy of eternal happiness and association with those gone before.

"She said she 'came to the gate of Paradise and saw my mother and my grandmother inside with their hands extended as if in greeting to her, but they did not speak—only beckoned her to enter.

"'The glory and brightness inside the gate was wonderful to behold,' and when she awakened it grieved her very much that she was back on earth again. I called to see her on Sunday evening, two days before she passed away. She was conscious, but in great pain, and constantly groaning in her anguish. She was pleased to have me read the scriptures, and in singing to her several hymns which she desired, her voice would unite with mine. Leading in prayer at her bedside, I asked God to remove from her the great pain, and to give her an easy transit from this world to the next. She instantly broke out with the cries of 'Come Lord Jesus, come quickly,' then she would sing 'O happy day when Jesus washed my sins away.' In all my past experiences in scenes like this I never saw any one so triumphant and happy over the anticipation of meeting their loved ones."

Her son wrote as follows: "On Sunday evening of November 17th she had a sinking spell; her limbs were cold and remained so for hours, notwithstanding artificial warmth and stimulants were used.

"Before she rallied from this her nephew, William A. Hall, came in, and after awhile, during which mother thought she was going, and had said, 'I love my children—I love you all; give my love and my good-byes to my brothers,' then when Will asked if he should sing, mother said 'Yes, Will.' Then he began Aunt Sarah's favorite hymn, 'When I Survey the Wondrous Cross,' and he had not reached the end of the first line before mother, with her poor, dear, feeble voice took up the tune and sang it to the end. Then Will read portions of the Psalms, and mother would repeat them after him, as only believers can who rely upon those promises.

"Then he prayed, and sang again 'O happy day when Jesus washed my sins away,' and again mother, with wonderful power, sang the entire hymn.

"After watching her for hours and hours

until Tuesday when, after seeing her suffer so much, I said 'Mother, I am resigned—better bear the pain of parting than to see you suffer,' and mother answered, ' Now take me Jesus, take me home.' Soon afterwards she fell asleep, and dozing and waking, but not to full consciousness, the time passed until nearly midnight, when, after two hours of unbroken rest, her breathing became shorter and feebler until she passed away.

"She had reached 'that goal of life where we lay our burdens down.'

"Then in a short time appeared the most wonderful transformation; the poor, pain-racked face lost every trace of sorrow and suffering, and took on a benignant, pleasant expression of twenty years ago.

"After the nurses and attendants had prepared her for the casket, she was beautiful, and on Thursday night, before the funeral services, Will's exclamation on seeing her was, 'That's my mother.'

" There was no crape upon the door, but a garland of roses instead.

"After the services of the church were read, and an address made by the rector, Rev. Lindsay Parker of St. Peters, of singular beauty and felicity, and old friends and new took their last farewells and adieus, there in the home made bright and sanctified by her pure presence, amid the sympathies of those who knew what a pilgrimage her sojourn had been, and amongst a wealth of lovely flowers that she always loved so well, it seemed as if sorrow were selfish and tears ingratitude."

The death of their Uncle Alanson Phelps in Ohio on November 5th, 1889, followed so quickly by the death of their only surving sister, brought great sorrow to all of the relatives in California, and on the day that the remains of Mrs. Griffiths were laid to rest in Greenwood Cemetery, at the suggestion of the eldest brother of Mrs. Griffiths, all of her brothers and their wives, and nearly all of her nephews and nieces, with a few personal friends, met at the house of William S. Phelps in San Francisco, and held a service in affectionate remembrance of the two dear friends who had so recently entered into rest. Upon invitation of the family Rev. Dr. A. W. Loomis, a Presbyterian clergyman, conducted the service, which consisted of reading selections of scripture, as well as the reading of some beautiful poems suitable to the occasion, accompanied with a few appropriate remarks, closing with a prayer and a benediction.

All who were privileged to be present felt that it was an occasion long to be remembered, and the memory of it is cherished by all of her brothers and their wives in California.

In looking over the relics and effects of his mother after her decease, Dr. Griffiths found several little poems among them, which his mother evidently had preserved for many years, and had probably read and re-read time and again until she probably knew them by heart.

To show the beautiful thoughts she cherished in her mind, a copy of one of them is inserted here, and will close this tribute of affectionate remembrance:

"ONLY REMEMBERED BY WHAT I HAVE DONE.

"Up and away like the dew of the morning
   That soars from the earth to its home in the sun,
So let me steal away gently and lovingly,
   Only remembered by what I have done.

" Gladly away from this toil would I hasten,
   Up to the crown that for me has been won,
Unthought of by man in rewards and praises,
   Only remembered by what I have done.

" Up and away like the odors of sunset
   That sweetens the twilight as evening comes on ;
So be my life—a thing felt but not noticed,
   And I remembered by what I have done.

"Needs there the praise of love-written record—
   The name and the epitaph graved on the stone?
The things we have lived for, let them be my story,
   We ourselves but remembered by what we have done.

" Not myself, but the truth that in life I have spoken;
   Not myself, but the seed that in life I have sown,
Shall pass on to ages—all about me forgotten
   Save the truth I have spoken, the things I have done."

CHAPTER XVII.

SARAH SOPHIA PHELPS, THE EIGHTH GENERATION.

Sarah Sophia Phelps, the third child and second daughter of Asa Hosmer and Margery (McCoun) Phelps, was born in Oyster Bay, Long Island, February 22d, 1823. Soon after her birth her parents removed to the city of New York, where she spent her early years, and attended such schools as were then carried on for young children in the city.

She was a girl of a lovely and amiable disposition, and early gave promise of maturing into a lady of beautiful appearance.

As already related in Chapter XII, at an early age she began to assist her mother in re-stringing beads as explained in the chapter referred to, and became an efficient helper to her mother in that labor.

The editor has received an account of her life written for this book by her eldest son, Mr. William A. Hall, of Brooklyn, N. Y., which is inserted here almost precisely as written by him. The article is as follows:

"Sarah Sophia Phelps was born at Oyster Bay, Long Island, in the year 1823. She came

SARAH SOPHIA PHELPS

(MRS. ISAAC HALL)

to New York City at an early age, and lived for several years at No. 158 Delancy street, where, under a mother's care and instruction, she grew to be a dutiful and loving daughter, and for the gentleness of her disposition and kindness of heart she was admired by all her associates. It was at this home that she became acquainted with a young man of English descent, named Isaac Hall, and the acquaintance ripened into love.

"He was a hard-working mechanic, just starting into business for himself as a shipsmith, and believing that with a wife like Sarah he would better his condition in life, they were married in New York City on September 1st, 1842. The young couple commenced life in humble circumstances, occupying small apartments in the lower part of New York, but it was not long before they were enabled to obtain a better home.

"Their children were:

"First. William Augustus Hall, born in New York, August 11th, 1843.

"Second. Sarah Louise Hall, born in New York, January 1st, 1845.

"Third. Isaac Hosmer Hall, born in Brooklyn, September 6th, 1846.

"Fourth. Ida Frances Hall, born in Brooklyn, September 26th, 1854.

"A short time after the birth of his second child Mr. Hall's affairs were in such a prosperous condition that he was able to purchase a home in Bergen street, Brooklyn. By a conscientious and industrious life the couple were enabled to give their children a good education, and they attended the best schools.

"After living a few years in Bergen street, Mr. Hall purchased a much larger house in a better part of the city, and moved his family to Dean street, where his youngest child, Ida Frances, was born.

"The family, now consisting of four children, received from their parent's teachings an influence for good which has followed them all these years. It was in this home that Sarah became a convert to the Christian faith, and united with the Strong Place Baptist Church, her husband being a member for many years of the orthodox Society of Friends. But it was in the dispensation of God's providence that a separation should come, and that the home associations should be sundered, and for two years Sarah suffered severely from an incurable disease, which she bore with patient faith, until on the 15th day of April, 1861, she passed to a better world, in her 38th year, sincerely mourned by her husband, her children, and her many friends.

"Her life, though a comparatively short one, was not devoid of many incidents showing her integrity and Christian traits of character.

"By her cheerful disposition and her spirit of hospitality she gathered about her home many friends. The loving care she ever manifested for her children endeared them to her, and the remembrance of the happy days they spent with her has been a benediction of love upon their lives. Her husband gratified every wish and desire of his devoted wife, and during her last illness his mind was constantly on her, studying and using every means possible towards securing the best obtainable medical advice.

"The memory of their mother's prayers in behalf of her children, her sympathetic and benevolent nature, her admonitions and advice, have been to her children a pleasing remembrance all the years since she was translated to her heavenly home.

"When Christ went with his disciples on Mt. Hermon, it was evident in the transfiguration of our Lord, that Moses and Elijah knew Him, and that the disciples knew those holy beings were Moses and Elijah; hence may we not assume that this is conclusive evidence that the spirits of those who are gone from us, are interested in the well-being of their loved ones who are engaged in the Lord's work on the earth?

"In the mind of every Christian believer there can be no doubt of this. So the many years that have passed since our mother has been separated from her loved ones in the flesh, yet in her spirit we believe she is alert to every act which pertains to God's kingdom, which they do."

As the foregoing writer has observed, Mr. and Mrs. Hall were members of different religious bodies. Mr. Hall, by a long line of ancestry back in England, being an Orthodox Friend, while Mrs. Hall was a Baptist, but they lived very happily together, and never had trouble over their religious views. He often accompanied her to church, and she frequently went with him to Friend's meeting.

He was a large and distinguished looking man, six feet or more in height, and a man of great business ability, and amassing a considerable fortune they were able to live in great comfort and affluence during the last few years of her life. She was a lovely woman—a very beautiful woman—of large and fine presence, a refined face with blue eyes and soft, brown hair, an agreeable and cordial manner, and possessed an excellent taste in dress which her husband's means enabled her to gratify; a kind and charitable friend, a loving and indulgent mother to her children, an affectionate daughter, and a generous sister to her brothers and her sister. She was a true and conscientious Christian, and adorned her profession as a disciple of Jesus Christ.

These things the editor writes from personal remembrance of both Mr. Hall and his wife, as they were exceedingly kind to him when he was a young man, and not only to him but to his mother as well, to whom they furnished a home for many years, and it gives him peculiar pleasure to put upon record, for preservation, this commemoration of their kindness, and in affectionate recollection of them.

It may be said of her as Milton speaks of Eve:

"Grace was in all her steps, heaven in her eye,
In every gesture dignity and love."

When she entered into Paradise may we not believe that had she been permitted to speak to us that she might have spoken these words of comforting

RECOGNITION.

The night is past, the sunrise comes
    Luminous o'er the sea,
Wafting a balm from glorious homes
    Waiting for you and me;
Waiting for us to enter in
    To breathe that fragrant balm,
Where twinge of pain, no taint of sin
    Defiles that holy calm.

There will be, recognition blest
    Amid the palms that wave,
Beyond the Sea, when we shall rest
    Exultant o'er the grave,
For, the Apostle Paul has said,
    In words that plainly bear,
"We shall, when risen from the dead
    All sit together there."

Upon the Shore, a Saint, I see
In raiment softly white,
    He scans the verge—he beckons me
With features of delight;
    It is my father; now I know,
What was so dark to me,
    When in the flesh I dwelt below—
This Heav'nly mystery.

Others I see, a happy shout
   Of welcome fills mine ear,
My friends I loved group me about,
   Dear ones I lost are here.
I praise my Maker for His love,
   This joy to me is given,
To meet upon this Shore above,
   And *know* my friends in Heaven.

AUGUSTUS ELIPHALET PHELPS

CHAPTER XVIII.

AUGUSTUS ELIPHALET PHELPS, THE EIGHTH GENERATION.

Augustus Eliphalet Phelps, the fourth child and second son of Asa Hosmer and Margery (McCoun) Phelps, was born in the city of New York, May 2d, 1825. Previous to the age of 10 years he attended the common schools of the city of New York, and the writer has often heard him relate with great humor the capers he used to perpetrate to avoid going to school, and how he used to play "hookey," and the consequent punishment inflicted therefor, not only by his teachers, but by his mother as well.

When he became 10 years of age his mother sent him to live with an old friend of the family, a Mr. Henry Fleet of Oyster Bay, Long Island.

A few months later his father died. He remained an inmate of Mr. Fleet's family six years, and attended the district school in the town during the winter months, and worked on and around the farm as such boys in the country are expected to do.

When 16 years of age he returned to New York to live with his mother, and soon afterwards commenced to learn the bookbinding trade with the great publishing house of Harper & Brothers.

He worked for them until he became master of his trade, and then continued with them as a journeyman until 1848, living with his mother, who then kept house in Delancy street. In the year 1848 he started a newspaper stand in Brooklyn and followed that business until the spring of 1849, when he suffered a very severe attack of the California fever, which was then virulently raging throughout the eastern States.

Allying himself with seventeen other young men of adventurous spirit, they formed a company of eighteen, bought the schooner "General Worth," of 175 tons, paying $9000 for her, and fitted her out for a voyage to the golden shores of California.

They sailed from New York on the 11th day of April, 1849; stopped at Rio Janiero, rounded Cape Horn, made a call at Valparaiso, and arrived at San Francisco October 15th, 1849, thus making him a Pioneer of the State. Here the company as a company broke up, although a few remained with the vessel, Augustus among the number. They almost immediately commenced running the schooner as a packet for passengers and freight on the Sacramento River, charging $30 for passage, and $80 per ton for freight from San Francisco to Sacramento.

He followed this business until the spring of 1850. In the spring of the latter year he went to try his fortune in the mines, going to what were then called the Southern Mines, in Mariposa county, where he met with fair success for about two months, when he returned to San Francisco. In the summer of 1850, with two partners, they bought a half interest in the scow "Brooklyn," and again went into freighting, this time from San Francisco to Alviso, the entrepot of San José. The venture was profitable, the scow sometimes making $3000 in a single trip.

During a part of the year 1851 he was employed by a contractor by the name of Ballentine, to oversee the laying of brick work.

In November of 1851 he returned to New York, going by the then newly-opened Nicaragua route, and from the date of his arrival in New York he remained in the city, visiting among his relatives and friends, until the following May, when he came to California, accompanied by his brother, William S. Phelps, as related in Chapter XV.

Upon the commencement of the business of Fick & Phelps, as also detailed in the chapter referred to, he commenced to learn the shipsmithing business, and worked faithfully at the forge until he had acquired a full and practical knowledge of the business, and when the firm of Fick & Phelps was dissolved, William took him into partnership as already stated, under the name of William S. Phelps & Co.

They were eminently successful and soon

acquired a fine reputation for excellent workmanship in their line of business, all up and down the Coast, which reputation they maintained all the days of his life.

He continued with his brother until the spring of 1857, when he returned again to New York, and on the 8th day of June, 1857, he was married in the city of New York to Miss Sarah E. McFarran.

She was the daughter of James and Sarah (Ayres) McFarran, and was born in New York City, April 18th, 1827.

They sailed for California on the 6th day of July, and safely arrived in San Francisco on the 31st day of July, 1857.

He took his wife to the house of his brother on the southwest corner of Jones and Pacific streets, and in a few weeks thereafter they (he and his wife) commenced housekeeping in the upper part of the house that William was then living in.

The children of Augustus and Sarah (McFarran) Phelps were:

First. Anna Phelps, born in San Francisco, July 20th, 1858, and died July 20th, 1858.

Second. Asa Hosmer Phelps, born in San Francisco, October 28th, 1859.

Third. Warren Phelps, born in San Francisco, June 21st, 1861, and died October 17th, 1862.

Fourth. Frank Augustus Phelps, born in San Francisco, July 23d, 1865.

Fifth. Frederick Phelps, born in San Francisco, July 23d, 1865, and died July 23d, 1865.

He lived in the upper part of the house above mentioned until the latter part of the summer of 1858, when he removed to a house which he had purchased immediately adjoining the house of his brother, and which house he continued to occupy until its removal to the east side of Jones street, in 1880, as related in Chapter XV.

Following the example of his elder brother, in the year 1865 he joined the order of Free and Accepted Masons on November 27th of that year, and maintained his membership in Golden Gate Lodge No. 30 as long as he lived.

In 1863, during the war of the rebellion, fired with an ambition to do what he could to show his loyalty to his country during her great struggle, he joined Company A (light battery of artillery) of the California militia, and faithfully drilled and served as a private for over one year. The battery at that time was commanded by Captain Isaac Bluxome, a man who occupied a very conspicuous position during the days of the great Vigilance Committee of San Francisco, and his company at that time was filled with young men who served as Mr. Phelps did— because of love for their country.

By reason of his early arrival in California he was eligible as a member of the Society of California Pioneers, and with the belief in mind that that society was one that would perpetuate the history and the noble achievements of the Pioneers of the State, of which, as a Pioneer, he was very proud, he made application to, and was duly admitted as a member of the society on the 21st day of July, 1868.

From the first he took great interest in it, and on the 7th day of July, 1888, he was elected a director of it, and was continually re-elected every year thereafter up to and including the year of his death, and held the office at that time.

He was a man who took great pleasure in social matters, such as the Society of Pioneers afforded, and he was an efficient and a valuable member, a man of good judgment and executive ability, of pleasant conversational powers, and who knew how to arrange pleasant functions for an organization of that kind.

He also possessed a genial disposition and manner, and in his family he loved to meet his friends, and to gather them around his table.

He knew how to cater for a large number of people at one time, and there was no pleasure in life which he enjoyed more than to have a table full of congenial friends come to dine with him, and to see them enjoy the good things his taste and hospitality had furnished for their entertainment. His acquaintance being very large, especially among seafaring men with whom his business brought him in close and frequent contact, he was enabled to obtain many delicacies from domestic and foreign places that ordinary men find it hard to procure, and he was always on the alert to get good things to eat, as well as curios from many foreign parts.

He was a man who never forgot his friends, and he was constantly doing little kindnesses to them—a man who loved to give gifts because of the pleasure he experienced in seeing those he loved made happy.

He was a great admirer of children and young people, and liked to have them visit him, and to do for them as he often did for his older friends in the way of hospitality.

In fact his character may be summed up in a few words: he was a man of large and generous heart, with no room in it for petty meannesses.

The editor is under obligation to Franklin M. Farwell, Esq., of Saratoga, Santa Clara county, California, for the following account, which he has furnished for this book:

"I first knew Augustus E. Phelps in 1852, and from that time to his death was on intimate terms with him, so much so that he was known by our family as 'Uncle Gus.' We considered him one of our best friends, and we always found him a kind and generous man. He seemed to be really jealous of his friends, that they should have no friend as good, or any better than himself. I never saw a man who seemed more in his natural atmosphere than when surrounded with his friends in his own home, and in making them happy. In the spring of 1874 his brother-in-law, Mr. Isaac Hall, and wife, of Brooklyn, N. Y., were out to San Francisco on a visit to the brothers. At a social gathering of the family one evening at the home of Uncle Gus, a very funny scene occurred that I shall never forget. Mr. Hall, it seems, came from Quaker stock, and during the evening the Shaking Quaker burlesque dance that the celebrated Christy's Minstrels of New York made so popular about 1850 was talked of, and Mr. Hall proposed that we have a Quaker dance after the Christy Minstrel style, and that he would take the lead, and as all of us had lived in New York and had seen the Christys do the dance, we all entered into the spirit of it heart and soul. Mr. Hall selected five of us as follows: W. S., A. E., and A. H. Phelps, Lyman Grimes, and myself, making six in all.

"We all took off our coats, and followed behind Mr. Hall in single file around the double parlors, singing what was called the 'Fi-hi-hi chorus,' in a sort of monotone voice, and moving with short, jiggling steps, our elbows against our sides, and our hands with their palms downward, and with limp wrists, the position of the Shaking Quakers.

"We followed around the room several times, and then we filed three abreast up and down the center of the room behind each other, and in coming back did not face about, but would back up.

"On the first line was Mr. Hall, Uncle Gus and A. H. Phelps. After we had jogged up and back two or three times, as we were all backing up, William S. Phelps threw himself, quick as a flash, on the floor behind the first line. Mr. Hall's heels struck William's body, and over he tumbled backwards; then came A. H. P. on top of Mr. Hall, and next Uncle Gus began to topple over backwards, and yet so slowly that I had time to take in the tableau, with his corpulent figure, with hands instinctively thrown above his head, his feet left the floor slowly, and he cushioned on top of the pile, with arms and legs in the air at the same time. It was the most graceful fall for a large body I ever saw, and did not hurt him in the least. William was still under the mass of bodies, swinging legs and arms, whose individual ownership to the spectators was for a time somewhat uncertain, and being in our shirt sleeves made the scene more comical, with the surrounding friends laughing and dancing around this struggling pile, a picture in my mind never to be forgotten. Grimes and myself kept out of the jam, but kept on our feet, and from our position I think we saw more of the fun than those in front."

Mr. Phelps was a man who dearly loved such social gatherings, and in the early years of his married life, before he became so very stout, he often gave social parties in his spacious rooms, to which his friends were always welcomed with a hearty and generous good will.

Although he never made any profession of religion, yet he was always a supporter of the church by giving constantly in support of it, by having a pew, and in contributing in that way for the support of the Gospel, and was often an attendant on divine service.

In the autumn of 1889 he was seriously hurt on board of a ship by an injury to one of his limbs, which resulted in a severe illness to him, and which kept him in his house for several months, and from that time he was never again so strong and hearty as he was before the accident.

In a few months, however, he recovered so as to be able to attend to his business, but he never was really well again.

He died very suddenly and unexpectedly to his family and friends on the 15th day of October, 1892, on the forty-third anniversary of his arrival in California, after an illness of only about twelve hours, the immediate cause of death being fatty degeneration of the heart. He was an extremely stout man, weighing at the time of his death about 280 pounds.

On account of an almost inexcusable mistake in the diagnosis of his disease by the physician who was called to see him early in the morning of the day of his death, neither himself, his own family, nor his brothers were informed as to the serious nature of his malady.

The doctor visited him three times from about 7 A. M. to 3 P. M., and not until the last visit did he surmise that Mr. Phelps could not long survive. Because of this ignorance of his physician the day was permitted to pass without any knowledge on the part of his own family, or by those of his brothers, that his end was so near.

The writer returned home from his business at about 5 P. M., and was at once informed that his brother was dying. He hastened to his side, but when he reached the room he was unconscious, and passed away within a few minutes.

His funeral was held under the auspices of Golden Gate Lodge of F. and A. Masons, in King Solomon's Hall, in the Masonic Temple, San Francisco, on Tuesday afternoon, November 18th, 1892.

There were twelve pallbearers—four representing the family, four from the lodge, and four from the Society of California Pioneers.

Besides a large number of Masons there was a delegation of Pioneers, numbering sixty-four, in attendance.

The service in the hall was conducted by the Master of the lodge, Edward L. Meyer, Esq. The male quartet of the Masonic order sang "Come to Me," "Abide With Me," and " Good Night."

The service at the grave was concluded by the reading of prayers by the Rev. David McClure, D. D., an Episcopal clergyman.

The funeral was a notable one because of the great number of people in attendance, crowding the large hall in every part and all the anterooms.

It was also notable because of the fact that all, or nearly all, were warm and personal friends of the deceased, and their presence served to testify their respect for him as a man and a friend.

Among the many floral gifts was a wreath of heliotrope and roses—heliotrope being a favorite flower of Mr. Phelps'—and attached to the wreath was a card bearing these lines from a poem by Wadsworth:

> "Like clouds that rake the mountain summits
> Or waves that own no curbing hand,
> How fast has brother followed sister
> From sunshine to the sunless land."

He sleeps in Laurel Hill Cemetery upon an eminence whose crest overlooks the broad Pacific, and above his grave there rolls the never-ending requiem of the sea.

ALANSON HOSMER PHELPS IN 1878

CHAPTER XIX.

ALANSON HOSMER PHELPS, THE EIGHTH GENERATION.

Alanson Hosmer Phelps, the fifth child and third son of Asa Hosmer and Margery (McCoun) Phelps, was born in Essex street, in the city of New York, on February 10th, 1832. He has but little remembrance of his early years in New York, but he can recall that he attended a little school for very small children. As heretofore related, his father died when Alanson was less than 4 years of age, but before his death he had arranged with his wife that one of his boys should be sent to Ohio, in due time, to live with his favorite sister, Aurelia, who was then the wife of Pliny Case.

In the fall of the year 1837 a merchant of Wayne, Ashtabula county, Ohio, a Mr. Clapp, went to New York to buy goods for his business, and it was mutually agreed between the mother of the subject of this sketch and the aunt, that Alanson should be the boy who should go to Ohio. Mr. Clapp came and saw Mrs. Phelps, and when he was ready to start on his return (to Ohio) the little boy's outfit of clothing was ready for the journey. When the day came for parting with him, his mother, and sisters, who were then just arriving at the age of womanhood, parted with him with many tears, as he was going out into the then wilds of a new country, of unknown dangers to them. His sisters fixed him up, combed and parted his hair, and he went away with Mr. Clapp into the great world,—into the wilderness of Ohio—as it were, alone, a little less than 6 years of age, to meet his fortune and his fate. At that time there were no railroads known. The journey had to be made by the Hudson River to Albany, and thence over the great Erie Canal to Buffalo. He remembers nothing of the journey up the Hudson, but he does remember that Mr. Clapp slapped him one day at the table on the canal boat for some childish misdemeanor. They took passage at Buffalo and went up Lake Erie to Cleveland, where they landed.

He remembers going up a street in Cleveland that seemed very wide to him, and also of seeing the stumps of trees still standing in the street. From Cleveland he was sent to Hudson, Ohio, which is about twenty miles from the former place, to meet his Uncle Alanson, who was then a student in the Western Reserve College, located in Hudson.

There he met his uncle for the first time, and remained with him a few days, until an opportunity offered to send him on his way to his aunt in Wayne. The opportunity came very soon by the visit to Hudson of a Congregational minister, a Mr. Latham, from Wayne, to whom the little boy was consigned to take to Wayne.

They left Hudson in a one-horse vehicle, and the boy well remembers the journey, or at least a part of it, where they went through dense woods, and where the road was full of mudholes, and covered with water.

As Hudson is about fifty miles from Wayne they must have staid over night at some place, but the little boy cannot remember where.

They arrived safely at last at the home of an aunt of the boy—his Aunt Malinda—who was married to Gamaliel Wilcox. Here he was received with affection and kindness by his aunt, as well as by his paternal grandparents, who then lived with her.

Word was sent to his Aunt Aurelia, who lived about three and a half miles away, and in a day or two his Uncle Pliny Case came after him, and taking him in front of him on horseback, carried him to his future home. Upon arrival at the house of his uncle he found a little cousin, the daughter of his uncle, standing out in front of the log house in which she lived, mounted on a pile of logs of wood and intensely watching for the little stranger from New York.

Upon arrival at the house he was received by his aunt with affection, accompanied with tears.

They arrived in the forenoon, and soon after dinner little Harriet asked the boy if he would not like to go out with her in the orchard and get some peaches, which were ripe at that time, and taking him out told him to pick some from a tree; this he objected to do, as he said "We don't pick peaches from a tree where I live; we buy them at a store."

This was repeated by little Harriet, and seemed very funny to all the family.

A short distance down the road from Uncle Pliny's lived Horace Wilcox, a brother of Uncle Gamaliel Wilcox, who had settled on a farm adjoining that of Uncle Pliny's, and during the afternoon Harriet took the lad to see the little Wilcox children, of whom there were four at that time—two girls and two boys—one of the boys being almost the same age as the subject of this sketch.

I remember with what interest they looked at him when his cousin brought him to their house to see them. This family of children afterwards were among his warmest friends, and his association with them for many years was a happy thing for the little boy.

And now there opens to the boy a new world and a new environment in life, and the bitter frown of poverty and incessant toil fell upon him and followed him through all his childish and youthful years.

The family of his uncle, at that time, was as follows: Uncle Pliny and Aunt Aurelia Case, their little daughter Harriet then nearly 5 years old, a younger brother of Uncle Pliny named Lauren Case, a daughter of Uncle Harvey Phelps named Anna Phelps, and a young boy named Maverick Wakeman.

The little boy was never adopted by his uncle and aunt; simply went to *live* with them, and as it was the opinion of his uncle that the chief end of a boy was to work and earn his living, he began at once to inculcate that doctrine in the mind of the boy, and he set him at work in the barn husking corn, giving him a stint to do each day—to husk so many baskets full of corn in a day or half a day. One day he gave him such a stint—to husk two two-bushel baskets full of ears during the forenoon. The work naturally became tiresome, and as there was a pile of ears on the floor already husked, the little chap helped out the stint by partially filling the basket from the pile on the floor.

This, of course, was contrary to his uncle's orders, and when the latter came in and saw the pile he knew that some deceit had been practiced, and accused the boy of it, and also accused him of having lied about it by pretending to him that he had husked all the corn in the basket, the result being the boy was whipped for the deceit.

The writer thinks now the punishment was more than the boy was entitled to, under the circumstances, as the temptation was left open before him. He was then a small and delicate boy, and had never before been placed in a position where he had work given him to do, and he was then not quite 6 years old.

His aunt was less strict about working, but she was very strict on all moral and religious questions, as she had been brought up in a very rigid Puritanical school, and exacted the most implicit obedience on all religious matters.

The country in which they lived was an extremely heavily timbered district, a very new country at that time, and, of course, everybody lived in a primitive way. A few years before Uncle Pliny had taken up the farm on which he then lived, comprising about fifty acres of land, and commenced to clear it of the timber around his house.

This was a work of exceedingly heavy labor. To clear a piece of land of two or three acres in extent was a season's work for two men, that is to say, they had to cut down the timber in the winter and spring, and in the early summer, or as soon as the logs were dry enough to burn, they would haul them together with oxen, pile and burn them up, and by the 25th of July they would try to get the land in condition so they could sow a crop of turnip seed on it, to grow and ripen by the time the snow would fly in the fall.

So he had worked from year to year, and at the time of the arrival of the boy he had quite a tract cleared for cultivation.

Lauren Case, the younger brother of Uncle Pliny, was then, I think, about 20 years old.

Like a great many other young men he was sometimes thoughtless, and did things he ought not to have done, and yet with no intention of being unkind. To the little boy he was unkind without intending to be so, as he would lift him up by the ears about breast high, almost every night after supper, and as he did so he would say "There, Lanson, that will make your ears grow."

As has already been stated, they lived in a log house, with a broad door opening into the kitchen, which was bedroom and living-room as well. The house, as I remember it, had only one room, although there may have been two rooms. The hired men and the boys had to sleep up stairs, going up a ladder under the gable roof of the house, and in the winter the snow would sift through the cracks between the logs, and in the morning the beds would be covered with snow.

The younger children were put to bed in a trundle bed which was fixed to run under the bed of the old folks during the daytime, and could be pulled out at night.

The kitchen had an enormous fireplace at one end with a large iron crane, decorated with links and hooks for hanging the different iron pots and kettles used for family cooking. The fireplace was long and deep, with large andirons, on which were placed great logs of wood.

The door into the house was very wide, so as to permit the boys to draw wood for the great fireplace into the kitchen on their hand-sleds, which I have done many times.

The fireplace also had a smooth hearth made of stone, and during the long winter evenings the family would gather around it and crack hickory nuts, eat apples and drink cider.

I was sent to the district school for a short time after I arrived there during the summer months, and during the winter, but my services were too valuable to my uncle for that long to continue, and after a year or two I was not permitted to attend school except for three months in the winter of each year. During the summer months I was kept busy riding horse to plow corn; to help in logging and other heavy work; to drive oxen to plow, without shoes to wear, with the result that my feet were constantly filled with the thistles which overran all the country at that time.

Uncle Pliny had what was called a "sugar bush," being a grove of maple trees which he used to "tap" every spring, from which he made a great deal of maple sugar. In those days they had to manufacture their own sugar or go without sweetening for cooking, as there was no cane sugar at that time.

The trees were "tapped" on the side about three feet from the ground, and a small wooden dug-out trough was placed under each tree to catch the sap, which was led into a trough by a bass-wood spout.

It was then gathered each day, or as often

as the troughs were filled, by going around among the trees with a pair of oxen hitched to a sled on which was a barrel, and the sap was gathered up and taken to the "camp," where there was an iron kettle set in stone work, in which the sap was boiled down to a thick syrup. After this was done it was then "sugared off," an operation of surpassing interest to the small members of the family. In "sugaring off" there is a time just before the sugar is cooked enough to "grain" when it gets cold, when, if taken out and placed on snow or ice, it forms a beautiful "wax," and at that time it is the best to eat of any time during the whole operation.

When Uncle Pliny opened his sugar bush the spring after my arrival, of course Maverick, Harriet and myself were on hand when the first "batch" of sugar was ready to be finished.

At the time there was some little snow left on the ground in spots, enough so that a handful could be obtained on which to drop some of the hot sugar to make the wax spoken of.

When the sugar was done enough to wax, Maverick went and got a handful of snow so that he could make some wax. I saw him do it and, of course, I wanted some. I went and got a handful of snow and brought it to Uncle Pliny, who then dipped out a generous supply on top of the snow.

It was boiling hot, but I did not know that it would burn me, as I thought the snow would cool it at once, so I put it to my mouth, the result being that I was most fearfully burned on my lips and on the inside of my mouth. Neither Uncle Pliny or Maverick told me to be careful and not get burned, and as it was I was badly burned.

Uncle Pliny was always fond of a joke, and he always looked upon that as a fine joke on the boy from New York.

One day, probably the year following the above incident, at the time of sugar making a boy came to the sugar bush where Maverick and I were boiling the sap of the sugar trees, and showing us some little pieces of wood, said that he "could make fire with them."

This was a marvelous thing for any boy to attempt to do, and we were very anxious to see him do it, and stepping to the side of the log cabin in which we were he scratched one of the little sticks on the side of a beech log that had the bark peeled off, and in a moment he showed it to us all on fire.

This was what was then called a "loco foco" match, and it was the first friction match we had ever seen, and it seemed very wonderful to us at that time.

Before the invention of friction matches, if the fire in the house went out from any cause, the housewife had to send to a neighbor and get some "live coals" to renew her fire for cooking purposes.

This I remember to have done sometimes for my aunt when her fire had gone out.

The settlers in northeastern Ohio were principally "Connecticut Yankees," and were a hardy and industrious race of men and women.

To illustrate the courage, the stamina and the hardihood of the latter, the following incident is inserted here:

In the township of Johnson, which is ten miles south of Wayne, lived a family by the name of Tyrrell. A son of the family came to Wayne, and taking up a piece of land in the "woods," about a mile and a half west of Uncle Pliny's, built him a cabin and commenced clearing his land preparatory to making a home for himself.

Soon after he came there we often used to see his mother trudging by our house on foot on the way to visit her son.

She generally passed by in the forenoon and returned in the afternoon, thus making her trip a journey of twenty miles when she reached her home on her return. One day late in November, just at dusk, when a thick snowstorm was raging, the family saw old Mrs. Tyrrell go by on her way to visit her son. At that time there was no regular road from the county road through the woods to his place—only a trail which in a storm like that then raging would soon be obliterated by the snow.

It was remarked by some member of the family as she went by that "old Mrs. Tyrrell might get lost in trying to find her son's place in such a snow storm and on such a night as this."

Uncle Pliny kept an ear out so as to hear the old lady if she should get lost and should "holler." Sure enough, in about half an hour we all heard a series of weird and unearthly yells coming from the dark and otherwise silent woods. Uncle Pliny lighted a lantern, and putting on his mittens, started out for the edge of the timber about a quarter of a mile away. The old lady continued her "hollering," and I well remember with what thrills we (the younger members of the family) heard her calls coming through the wintry air, and we thought how dreadful it must be to be lost in the woods on such a night as that, and we wondered whether her son could hear her as well as we could, and if he would know by the voice if it was his own mother. When Uncle Pliny reached the edge of the woods he began to reply to her calls, and after they had answered each other back and forth a few times, a third voice joined in the hallooing. This was her son, who at last heard the shouting, and knowing that some one was lost, he joined in the chorus.

After a little they—the mother and son—began to answer each other back and forth, so that Uncle Pliny knew that her son knew it was his mother who was in trouble, and when he was satisfied as to that he returned home and left him to extricate his mother as best he might.

This he did after a while. A day or two afterwards we saw the old lady pass by the house on her way home to Johnson.

These traits of fearlessness, of hardihood and indomitable pluck, were characteristic of the pioneer women of the early days in the settlement of Ohio.

There was no aristocracy of wealth in that community—all were poor, and all were struggling with the forces of nature to make *a very poor* living. Money was exceedingly scarce. To get money enough to pay the yearly taxes was a conundrum many a poor old farmer found it hard to solve. Nearly all the business was done by barter. Merchants were obliged to trust their customers, and wait for their pay until the farmer could turn off his butter, his cheese, some fat hogs in the fall, or else take grain, wheat or corn, in payment for his goods.

Every farmer tried to raise everything his family consumed, so far as could be done. In nearly every town there were grist mills, that were run by water power, where the farmers could take their grain, wheat, corn and rye, and have the miller return him flour or meal, after taking out his legal allowance for "toll." Many a time have I ridden a horse to mill with a bag of grain, and having obtained a promise when it would be done, have had to go after it and get it on a certain day.

Postage was then 25 cents a letter, and was paid by the party who received it. Letters did not fly around the country in those days as they do now. It cost too much *cash* to indulge often in the delights of a social correspondence with absent friends, and a letter from friends once a year was quite as often as it was desirable to hear from them.

There were no ready-made shoes or clothes to be had, and in the fall of the year the local shoemakers had many a growl from youngsters, who were without shoes, when the snow was lying deep on the ground, when he had failed to have shoes that he had promised to have finished on "Saturday night," and had lamentably failed to keep his promise.

The home-made clothes, made by the women folks, were marvels of style and finish, but this can be said of them, that they were generally *large enough* to cover the person for whom they were intended.

When I arrived at Uncle Pliny's he had already become quite distinguished for his enthusiasm for the culture of good fruit, having one of the best orchards in the county at that time, composed of the finest varieties obtainable of apples, peaches, pears, plums and cherries.

Before the original timber on the soil had been largely cut off in the clearings, fruit grew very finely in that part of Ohio.

This was no doubt owing to the proper ingredients for the growth of fruit trees in the soil, and the absence of all noxious insects and worms which, in later years, have been the bane of orchard culturalists all over the country. He was quite an adept in the art of budding and grafting different kinds of fruit. He had apples and pears growing on the same trees, and I remember at one time he had an apple tree which produced fruit, one side of which was *sour* and the other side *sweet*.

I think this was done by taking a bud from a sour-apple tree, and a like bud from a sweet-apple tree, and by carefully splitting them and placing them together, and then in inserting the bud as a graft on the bough of a thrifty tree. The apples had a thin line around them longitudinally, showing the line of the two different acids in the fruit.

They were a curiosity, but of no practical use, only to show what could be done with Dame Nature if one is disposed to try.

In the spring of 1844 Uncle Pliny sold his farm in Wayne and bought another one about ten miles away, in the town of Greene, Trumbull county, and moved his family there in April, 1844. In the month of June following, my mother and my sister Sarah, Mrs. Isaac Hall, came to Ohio on a visit to my uncle and aunt. While they were there it was arranged between my mother and Uncle Pliny that when I became 16 years of age I should be sent to New York, as she wished me to learn a trade.

During the years of 1845-46, and the early part of '47, I lived with Uncle Pliny and assisted him in his farm work during the summer months, and attended the district school in the winters.

In the spring of 1847 my mother wrote that

she wanted me to come to New York to commence to learn the trade she had concluded I should learn—the ship-smithing trade—of Mr. Hall.

In July I was sent to Buffalo, N. Y., in the care of two young men who were going to Connecticut from Greene.

We left Conneaut, Ohio, on a steamboat one Sunday morning, and went down Lake Erie, and arrived at Buffalo that evening. I remember with what surprise I noticed the elegant clothes worn by the people whom I saw upon our arrival, and I was struck with astonishment when I saw a man connected with the hotel take from his pocket a handful of silver coin to pay one for something. I thought it was wonderful that a man could have so much money at one time.

From Buffalo I went to South Wales, about twenty-five miles from Buffalo, to meet my mother, who was then visiting her brother, Daniel McCoun.

We remained there several weeks, and until mother was ready to return to New York, which she did in August, accompanied by my brother, William S. Phelps. We left Wales—mother, William and myself—and went to Buffalo, from thence to Niagara Falls, where we spent the afternoon, and from there we went to Lewiston, on Lake Ontario, where we took a steamboat for Oswego, arriving there the following morning.

Remaining there over night, the next day we started for Rochester by canal boat. We had passage on what was called a "packet," which traveled at the rate of five miles per hour, being hauled by three horses, hitched tandem, and driven on the "tow-path" by boys or young men.

These packets were built so as to carry as many passengers as possible, with one long room in the bow of the boat, and the kitchen in the stern, the table, at meal time, being set down the middle of the room, and at night berths were made up along the sides of the cabin, in which the passengers were carefully stowed away in their little bunks.

Upon our arrival in Rochester we were transferred to a like packet on the great Erie Canal, and went from thence on to Schenectady. I think we were nearly five days making that distance. From Schenectady we were carried by railroad to Albany, a distance of eighteen miles.

This was my first railroad ride, and while I cannot remember very much about the construction of the cars or the engine, I know that they were very different from what they are now; but I do remember that we went at what we thought was a very rapid rate, making the distance to Albany in about one hour. From Albany we traveled down the Hudson by steamboat, and arrived in New York in the afternoon, and going at once to the house of Mr. Hall, I saw my sisters. Soon after arriving there I was set to work in the ship-smith shop of Mr. Hall. I had not then attained my growth, and the work was rather hard for me.

I worked but a short time when I was taken very sick with dysentery.

During my sickness I became very homesick to return to Ohio, and after my recovery my mother concluded to let me go back, and in November I was permitted to return there, accompanying two of my Uncle Daniel McCoun's sons from New York to Buffalo, and after visiting at Uncle Daniel's house a few days I went on to my destination alone, going up Lake Erie by boat, and landing at Fairport, Lake county, and thence to Uncle Pliny's by stage and wagon.

I was received by my Aunt Aurelia with great affection upon my return, and became one of the family at once. Having no son of her own, she looked upon me almost as if I were her own boy, and she was rejoiced when I came back to live with her. I entered at once upon the duties of a boy upon a farm, doing such work and chores as are always to be done where there are cattle and sheep to be cared for in the winter, and this continued almost all of the years of 1848, '49, '50, and a portion of '51, except that I attended a select school in Greene for about seven and a half months during the autumns of those years.

In the winters of 1850 and '51, however, I taught a small district school in Colebrook, Ashtabula county, Ohio, and earned the handsome salary of $12 per month, and had the felicity to "board around" among the parents of my scholars.

In the summer of '51 I worked at carpentering with a young man by the name of Linus A. Harrington. He was a young man of great versatility of mind—one of the few real humorists I have ever known.

The poor fellow came to California in the winter and spring of 1852, coming around Cape Horn in a sailing ship, but very soon after his arrival here he was taken sick and died soon after in the old St. Mary's Hospital on Stockton street, near Vallejo. After my arrival in San Francisco a friend took me on a Sunday morning to visit his grave, which was then in the old Yerba Buena Cemetery, situated where the City Hall of San Francisco now stands.

In the summer of 1853, in company with Aunt Aurelia Case, I went to New York City on a visit to my mother and sisters, and while there I saw the first World's Fair held in the United States, in New York City.

I also had the great pleasure to hear the great Julien with his wonderful orchestra of musicians in a grand concert held in Castle Garden.

It was the grandest music I had ever heard, and the memory of the occasion has never faded from my mind.

Returning to Ohio in the fall of that year, upon invitation of Uncle Alanson Phelps, I visited him and his family at Franklin Mills, Portage county, Ohio, where he was then the rector of an Episcopal Church.

After my arrival there he suggested that I take a school in the town of Franklin Mills for the winter months, and remain with him, and with his assistance I obtained a school at a salary of $22 per month. During the winter I attended a commercial school opened in the village, being a branch of Folsom's Commercial College of Cleveland, Ohio.

Uncle Alanson Phelps resigned the rectorship of the parish in the winter that I was there, and in May or June following he received a call to the rectorship of St. James' Church in Painesville, Lake county, Ohio, which he accepted, and moved his family there during the month of August, 1854. The year 1854 was notable because of the cholera which was then raging all over the country, and in Ohio as well. I accompanied my uncle's family to Painesville, as through his good offices I had obtained a situation as a clerk in the Bank of Geauga at that place, but owing to a severe illness, similar in effect to that of cholera, I was unable to hold the position except for a few weeks, and had to give it up after an illness that nearly ended my life. After I had recovered and was able to be around, and yet being unable to work, I returned to my Uncle Pliny's house in Greene, and spent the winter and spring in that town.

During a part of each of the years of 1855

and '56 I was clerking in two different country stores, the latter year in Colebrook, Ashtabula county. That was a year of a Presidential election—the year when General John C. Fremont was nominated for President on the Republican or Free Soil ticket, and my first vote for President was given to him.

In the month of May, 1857, having finished my term of clerking in Colebrook some time previous to May, and in answer to a request from my mother to come to New York, I left Ohio and went to New York, and spent the year 1857 with my mother and sisters there. As heretofore related, my brother Augustus returned from California to New York in the spring of that year, and after my arrival there he urged me to go back with him to California. This I would not then consent to do, as I did not then think that I cared to go to the Pacific Coast.

After his return to California he continued to write to me urging me to come. In the winter of 1857 and '58 I concluded to go to California, and on the 20th day of March, 1858, I sailed for the Pacific Coast on the steamer "Star of the West" of the Pacific Mail Steamship Line, for Aspinwall. On the Pacific side we took the steamer "Golden Age."

In these southern latitudes I saw for the first time the magnificent jewels in the constellation of the Southern Cross.

On the steamer were a number of distinguished people, among them General John C. Fremont and his family.

We arrived in San Francisco on the evening of April 12th, 1858, and my two brothers, Augustus and Daniel Phelps, met me at the wharf and took me to my brother William's house on the corner of Pacific and Jones streets.

Before my arrival my brothers had obtained a promise of a situation for me upon my arrival, from the then existing firm of Conroy & O'Connor, with whom my brothers were then trading for iron, but after my arrival they (Conroy & O'Connor) refused to make good the promise, the result being that instead of having a situation open for me I was without any means of immediately earning my living.

After a few weeks spent in the city I went to Sutter Creek, in Amador county, and went to work in a quartz mill for a few weeks, but returned to the city in the latter part of July. Early in August Brother William informed me that he had secured a position for me in the iron house of Thomas H. Selby & Co., and on the 10th day of August, 1858, I commenced as a clerk at a salary of $50 per month for the first four months, and was then advanced to $75 per month. I continued in the house of Thomas H. Selby & Co. during all the years of the life of Mr. Selby, which ended on the 9th day of June, 1875.

During the last part of the year 1858 I first

met the lady whom I subsequently married. She was then a Mrs. S. Frederick Sargent, and was then accompanying her husband, master of the bark "Jenny Ford," trading in the lumber business between Puget Sound and San Francisco.

During a trip to the port of Port Gamble, on Puget Sound, Captain Sargent lost his life by falling overboard from a vessel lying at the dock in that place. After the recovery of his body and its burial there, his widow returned to San Francisco, and upon her arrival my brother William met her and brought her to his house, where she spent a few weeks prior to her departure to her native place, Bangor, Maine, in the early spring of 1859.

In the year 1862 I opened a correspondence with her which resulted in an engagement of marriage between us, and on the 18th day of March she arrived here on the steamer "Constitution" from New York, via. Panama.

She was the daughter of Edward and Lettice Maxwell (Brown) Wiggin, and was born in Essex street, Bangor, Maine, on the 20th day of August, 1834.

On the 23d day of March, 1864, Alanson Hosmer Phelps and Ellen Bartlett Wiggin (widow of S. Frederick Sargent) were married in the house of Augustus E. Phelps, by the Rev. Edward S. Lacy, pastor of the First Congregational Church of San Francisco.

Their children were:

First. Albert Alanson Phelps, born in San Francisco, March 6th, 1867.

Second. Alice Maud Phelps, born in San Francisco, June 4th, 1869, and died March 18th, 1871.

Third. Roger Sherman Phelps, born in San Francisco, July 2d, 1876.

On the first day of May following the death of little Alice Maud Phelps, with my wife and little boy Albert, we left San Francisco on the Central Pacific train for Ohio, New York and Maine. After visiting our friends in Ohio in different places for a few days, we went to New York, and remaining there a few days. We then went on to Maine, arriving in Bangor, on the first day of June. I remained with the parents of my wife six days in Bangor, and then returned alone to New York via. Boston, leaving my family in Bangor. After a few days with my relatives in New York I left for California, stopping two days in Ashland Ohio. My mother came on from New York, and meeting her on the train at Mansfield, Ohio, we came on together towards California via. Chicago, Denver and Ogden, where she left me, going on alone to San Francisco, while I went to Salt Lake City. Upon my return to San Francisco a few days later, I resumed my position in the house of Thomas H. Selby & Co.

In a few weeks Mr. Selby wished me to go to Salt Lake, and with a nephew of his establish an office in that city for the purchase and shipment of lead and silver ores to his smelting works recently established in San Francisco. This we did, going there in August, 1871.

I remained there from August until about the middle of November following when I returned to the latter place, accompanied by my wife and son, who had returned from Maine in October.

Upon my return I was at once permitted to resume my old position in the store of Mr. Selby.

In the fall of 1865 I bought of Dr. Samuel Merritt the lot on Jones street, San Francisco, 137 feet and 6 inches south of the southeast corner of Pacific and Jones streets, and built my house thereon in the summer of 1866, and moved into it in the early part of October of the same year.

In that house all of my children have been born.

In the winter of 1865 Alanson H. and Ellen B. Phelps were admitted to membership in the Green Street Congregational Church of San Francisco, and continued members thereof until the summer of 1878, when they withdrew from it, and in the spring of 1880 they were both confirmed in the Grace Episcopal Church, San Francisco, by the Right Reverend William Ingraham Kip, Bishop of California, and we have been members of the Episcopal Church ever since. Under the rectorship of Rev. William H. Platt, D. D., I was elected a vestryman of Grace Church on April 18th, 1881, and was honored with a re-election every year from 1881 to 1894, and was continuously a delegate to the Diocesan Convention from said parish from 1885 to 1895, and was also a delegate from said parish to the special convention of the diocese called for the election of an assistant bishop to Bishop Kip, who had become superanuated, held in Trinity Church, San Francisco, in February, 1890, and voted for the successful candidate, the Rev. William Ford Nichols, D. D., of St. James' Church, Philadelphia.

In March, 1895, for reasons satisfactory to myself, I resigned the offices of vestryman (and junior warden of Grace Church, which office I had held continuously since April 21st, 1884), and in March, 1896, with my wife, we were transferred from Grace Church to St. Luke's, in San Francisco. At the Easter election of delegates to attend the Annual Convention of the Diocese of California to be held in Grace Church in May of 1896, I was elected a delegate to said convention, from St. Luke's, and served in that capacity.

In the winter or spring of the year 1862, with my brother, Augustus E. Phelps, I joined the First California Guard (light artillery) and served in the ranks for about one year. When the San José and San Francisco Railroad was completed and opened first for traffic, the people of San José had a celebration in honor of the opening of the road, and the California Guard were invited to go to San José and participate in the festivities. We went there on the first regular passenger train that ever ran over the road between San José and San Francisco, and carried our guns, and fired a salute at the opening of the road in February, 1864.

In the month of June, 1875, Edward Wiggin, the father of Ellen Bartlett Phelps, died in Bangor, Maine, and in November of the same year her mother, Mrs. Edward Wiggin, came to California and made her home with her daughter until her death on the 13th day of February, 1893.

Upon the death of Thomas H. Selby in June, 1875, the opportunity came for me to enter into business for myself, with Mr. Henry S. Austin and Mr. Edward Hammer as general partners, and with Mrs. Thomas H. Selby as a special partner, by the purchase of the goods and good will of the late firm of Thomas H. Selby & Co., and we carried on the business at the old store, 116 California street, for over six years, when there was a change on the 1st day of January, 1883, by the purchase of the interest of Mr. E. H. Hammer by the three other partners. The business was continued two years more at the same place under the same name.

On the 1st day of January, 1885, the interest of Mrs. Thomas H. Selby was purchased by Mr. Henry S. Austin and Alanson H. Phelps, and was then removed to Nos. 220 and 222 Mission street, where the business was carried on by the two gentlemen above named under the name of Thomas H. Selby & Co. until the first day of 1887, when it was changed into the firm name of Austin & Phelps, and was continued under that name until the tragic death of Mr. Henry S. Austin by a railroad accident in Oakland Creek on the 30th day of May, 1890.

In the month of February, 1877, the general agency for the Pacific Coast of the Hazard (Sporting) Powder Company was very unexpectedly tendered to the firm of Thomas H. Selby & Co., and was accepted by them, and was continued and carried on by them successfully, and by their successors.

After the death of Mr. Henry S. Austin, and the settlement of his estate in the spring of 1891, the business was continued under different auspices, including the agency of the Hazard Powder Company, until the 31st day of March, 1896, when, having disposed of nearly all my interest in the business at Nos. 220 and 222 Mission street, I retired from the firm and accepted the sole agency of the above company for the Pacific Coast on April 1st, 1896.

Owing to the undermining of my health, caused by too close application to business, I was advised by my physicians to take a long rest and vacation from business, and on July 13th, 1881, I left California with my wife and youngest son for the eastern States.

We visited Ohio, Niagara Falls and Saratoga Springs; Manchester, Vt., Portland and Bowdoinham, Maine, and finally reached New York and Brooklyn in October. During the visit I made a flying trip from New York to Philadelphia, Washington and Mount Vernon.

On our return we visited Pittsburgh, Pa., and Painesville, Ohio, and arrived home in San Francisco, December 4th, 1881.

In 1886 I was cheerfully and cordially invited to visit New York by the Hazard Powder Company at their expense, which I as cheerfully and cordially accepted, and on June 3d my eldest son and myself started for New York, going by the Central Pacific and Denver and Rio Grande Railways.

While away we visited Newport and Providence as the guests of the Hazard Powder Company. We also visited Keyport, Ocean Grove, Long Branch and Elberon, N. J., as the guests of Dr. Joseph B. Brown of Brooklyn.

On our return we visited Pittsburgh, Pa., Greene, Trumbull county, and Painesville, Ohio, and reached home on August 1st, 1886.

In response to a subpoena issued to me by the United States Marshall for the Northern District of California, it became my duty to appear in the U. S. District Court on the 15th day of February, 1895, when I was sworn in as a member of the United States Grand Jury to serve for the term commencing on that date.

After having been sworn as a member of said jury, Judge William W. Morrow then did me the honor to appoint me as Foreman of the jury and I was then sworn again to act in that capacity.

The jury convened immediately for business, and during the term we were in service I presided at 38 sessions of the jury, and we were finally discharged on the 3d day of July, 1895.

Who can explain the inexplicable? What metaphysician who has written the ablest treatise ever produced by man, upon the powers of the human mind, has been able to explain the mysterious forces which control our souls? Is there a connection of the material forces of this world with the spiritual forces of the world which lies beyond the vision of these mortal eyes? Do angels and the spirits of those who have preceded us to the hidden world around us have the power, when our minds are in a receptive and congenial state, to flash to us across the abyss that divides the immortal from the mortal world, some slight snatches of the knowledge they possess, and are we permitted to receive, by a glance, as it were, intelligence from them, and are we constituted so that we can use such intelligence in intellectual forms?

Have they power to fill our souls with sublime and lofty thoughts of great originality and beauty—thoughts that take complete possession of us and dominate us and compel us to do and to act as we never before have acted in all our lives? If such experiences do come to us in certain states of our minds, may we not justly believe that there is a connection between earthly souls and the angels of light, or with the souls of those who are in Paradise, and may not we rationally assume that God has endowed some human souls with the capacity to receive and to appropriate such revelations or inspirations from the world above?

The writer knew a man a few years ago who apparently had passed through such an experience. One Sunday morning while at divine service this message was instantaneously flashed into his mind: "You can write in poetical measures." It was an overwhelming surprise to him, and it found him utterly unprepared, by his modes of thought, and by the structure of his mind, to attempt anything in a rythmical form, and yet the message was so real to him that he determined to *try*, and to see what he could do by an actual test, and if he *did* possess any powers of versification. He was a business man who, for many years, had devoted all his attention to the details of his constant business. He was a comparatively illiterate man, having in his youth been favored with but slight educational advantages, and when this message came to him it found him with a mind entirely unadapted to the higher modes of thought requisite for literary work, even if he possessed the originality of mind to produce anything any one in the world would care to read, and he was loth to attempt the task. He had already passed his

54th birthday, and he had never suspected that he possessed any poetical powers.

The influence of the message, however, continued with him constantly; it did not fade away as he thought it would do, but it grew stronger as the days went on, and he became so impressed with the idea in his mind that he made an attempt at writing a few lines in rythmical form.

His first effort was very crude, as might be expected, because he had no practical knowledge of the construction of poetical feet—no knowledge of the accent that ought to be given in such writings, and had a poor knowledge as well of the rules of grammar. He had nothing of the felicity of expression that is required in the production of beautiful poetry. His mind was a barren field upon which the flowers of rhetoric and poetical feeling had never been suffered or encourage to grow.

He had read some of the works of the great poets of the century, and of the older poets, but he did not have an overshadowing love for poetry.

Without any real conception of what he was going to do he groped along uncertain as to what it all meant, until in a few days there began to appear in his mind groupings of words in sentences, and finally completer lines of remarkable import to him.

Thoughts that were absolutely new to him came to him in his daily business, or when walking to and from his business, and in the silent night, until there began to appear a regiment of new and beautiful thoughts which he saw needed to be marshaled in a metrical and poetical form. This he slowly attempted to do but he found it exceedingly difficult to arrange them in poetical measures.

The lines would not come out right—some were too long and some too short—and his first efforts were very discouraging, but he was induced, perhaps by a higher power, to persevere, and at last he saw that the matter forming in his mind was to be a poem relating to the world above, although when he commenced it he had no idea where it would lead him, or of its final completion, because he did not think or imagine that he had the ability to write on such a profound subject.

One night he was awakened about half-past two o'clock with a rush of overpowering and tumultuous thoughts—thoughts such as he had never experienced before. They came in regular order, in lines of a certain length and measure, and he was so impressed with them, with their construction, with their felicity of expression, that he arose from his bed, and lighting his room, took a pencil and paper, and at once wrote them off just as they had first appeared in his mind.

The lines were a portion of a poem that he subsequently composed, and the effusion was shortly afterwards published in a religious newspaper in San Francisco, the title of the poem being "A Dream of Heaven." The lines he wrote on that night of his life never-to-be-forgotten by him, were as follows:

>The gates of pearl swing out
>   The Golden streets appear,
>I see the homes of Paradise
>   Domed in the air.
>
>Within I see my friends
>   I knew on earth while here,
>Conscious of their felicity
>   They wish me there.
>
>I see mine own child there,
>   Eyes innocent of tears,
>Clad in celestial textures,
>   Now, a crown she wears.
>
>They signal me to come
>   Within the City walls,
>Communion sweet with me to hold
>   Ere my evening falls.
>
>There every hope and wish
>   Full gratified must be,
>To all who have attained unto
>   That blest Eternity.
>
>In consonance with their wish
>   Inciting me to come,
>A cymbal rings in ecstacy
>   To win me home.
>
>I see, I hear the call,
>   I yearn to enter there,
>While yet my vile mortality
>   Doth bind me here.

These lines came to the house of his soul when there was no expectancy of receiving such guests, and no preparation had been provided for their entertainment.

They came to his soul and they found it like a seed of a rare and exquisite plant which by some misfortune in its youth had been cast out of its natural home in the garden of a Prince, and had been swept away, far away, where it had fallen into the dry and sterile soil of a desert, where it had striven to obtain a precarious life— where it had been twisted, and bent and gnarled and dwarfed by the dessicating winds of the fierce sirrocos that beat upon its life; there it lived outcast and alone, until one day the Prince himself was crossing the desert, when he saw the little plant lifting up its humble head in the arid wastes.

He at once recognized it; he knew its heredity; he knew that if it were transplanted to a fertile and generous soil it would, in due time, with its wealth of beauty, repay the toil of its transference from the desert to his garden. He called one of his retinue of servants and directed him to take the plant and carefully carry it home to his garden; to plant it in a generous place, where the sun and the air would fructify it; to enrich the soil about it with fertilizing wealth; to straighten its crooked stem by training it to stand upright; to prune away all of its knotty protuberances; to cut away all of its dead limbs and leaves; to watch it day by day as it began to unfold a new crown in the air, and that some morning he would come, when lo and behold! there would appear upon its stem a blossom of supernal beauty, fresh with the bloom and the odors of Eden.

DANIEL TOWNSEND PHELPS

CHAPTER XX.

DANIEL TOWNSEND PHELPS, THE EIGHTH GENERATION.

Daniel Townsend Phelps, the sixth child and fourth son of Asa Hosmer and Margery (McCoun) Phelps, was born in the city of New York, April 21, 1835. His father died a few months after he was born. He attended some of the little schools in New York City in his early years, and when he was 9 years of age his mother sent him to South Wales, Erie county, New York, to live with and be brought up by his maternal uncle, Daniel McCoun, after whom he was named.

Here, when he became old enough, he worked around the farm of his uncle during the summer months, and attended the district school in the winter. When he became older he assisted his uncle in his sawmill work, and also frequently drove a team of horses with wagons loaded with lumber to Buffalo, N. Y., where Mr. McCoun sent large quantities of ash and hemlock for sale, the distance being about twenty-five miles.

When Daniel had reached his 17th year his mother made arrangements with her son-in-law, Isaac Hall, to take him as an apprentice in his shop to learn the ship-smithing trade, and he then went to New York, and entering the shop of Mr. Hall, commenced to learn the trade, making his home with his employer all the time he was working as an apprentice.

After he became master of his trade he continued to work for Mr. Hall for wages until the spring of 1857 when, at the solicitation of his brothers in San Francisco, he started for California, by the Isthmus route, having been offered a position in the shop of his brothers.

He arrived in San Francisco early in the spring of the year above mentioned, and immediately entered the shop of his brothers as journeyman ship-smith, boarding with his brother Augustus until his marriage, and a short time time after his marriage.

On the 23d of November, 1864, he was married in the First Baptist Church in San Francisco, by the Rev. Dr. D. B. Cheney, to Miss Eliza Jane Donnellan. She was the second daughter of Benjamin Crockett and Eliza (De Guerre) Donnellan, and was born in Iowa, April 14th, 1846.

They have had no children.

On June 27th, 1870, Daniel Townsend Phelps was admitted as a member of Abou Ben Adhem Lodge, I. O. O. F., in San Francisco, and has maintained his membership in that lodge ever since, and in his life has followed the motto of his lodge, as follows:

"Write me as one who loves his fellow men."

He is a man of quiet and unassuming life, a hard-working, steady man, and has always had the respect and esteem of his neighbors and acquaintances.

For many years he lived in the immediate vicinity of the homes of his brothers in San Francisco, but a few years since he purchased a home on Dorland street, near Eighteenth, and there he is spending the later years of his life.

CHAPTER XXI.

A TRADITION OF THE FAMILY.

The following tradition was sent to the writer of this book in the year 1888 by R. T. Servin, Esq., of Lenox, Mass.

The relationship of the writer of the tradition to our branch of the family being that of first cousin to Grandfather Eliphalet Phelps:

"A short narrative of our ancestors, as handed down to us from our forefathers; not by any authentic records, but verbally, from generation to generation down to the writer's own time, and as received from my father, who lived until he was about 95 years of age, and in a measure retained his reason to the last.

"About the year 1616, when King James I. was on the throne of England, there had arisen a religious sect, called by some Nonconformists, by others Puritans. This sect refused to make use of all the ceremonies and fooleries, as they termed them, which were made use of in the religious meetings of the established church, which was Episcopalian.

"For this they were persecuted to such a degree that the Rev. Mr. Robertson, with most of his congregation, removed to Holland and settled themselves in the city of Leyden. In this society were two young men by the name of Phelps, and it appears that these two brothers were the ancestors of all of this name that have ever been or are now in America; for we have never learned that any other one of our name has set foot upon American ground. After a very few years this company found themselves in no better situation than when in England, and they determined once more to rid themselves of their persecutors, and this by crossing the Atlantic Ocean, and seat themselves down in the wilds of America, where they could worship God according to the dictates of their own consciences, without any one to molest or make them afraid in religious matters. It was agreed that only a part of the company should go first and prepare for themselves and those that remained, the best accommodations in their power, and this last squad should join the first company the next year. The society hired a Dutchman as captain, together with a ship called the "May Flower," to transport these first emigrants to the mouth of the North River (where the city of New York now stands), but on account of many hindrances they did not hoist sail for this voyage until the sixth day of September, one thousand six hundred and twenty. On account of the lateness of the season and rough weather on their passage, they did not reach America until December, and either through ignorance or treachery of the captain, the first land they made was Cape Cod, far north of the Hudson River, where he landed his passengers, and immediately left them to take care of themselves.

"Here they were in a wilderness country, and winter having already set in, with snow on the ground, not a white person to be seen except themselves, but surrounded by wild Indian tribes.

"These emigrants kept up worshiping God on the Sabbath, as also morning and evening prayers while on board ship, likewise after landing at the Cape. There seemed to be a particular Providence in preparing the Indian chief that was in this neighborhood for the reception of this handful of whites. By giving him a few presents of English manufacture which, being of little value, notwithstanding were considered of great value by him, and these, with some few others, obtained his friendship during his long life.

"The chief's name was Massasoit, and he had command of all the tribes that surrounded these pilgrims. He not only assisted them with his own hands, but directed his subjects to give these strangers all the assistance that was in their power; and, in fact, many of these natives did assist these whites in building their temporary huts, or wigwams.

"In the winter and spring these Indians helped these strangers to provisions, etc., and, indeed, had it not been for the help they received through the influence of this good and great chief, it is thought by many, that they must have perished with hunger.

"Several of these Englishmen were taken sick before they left the ship, and after landing others were taken down; and not long after the sick began to die, and the disease raged to such a degree that by the middle of May following nearly one-half of their number were in their graves. From this time forward the sickness abated, and soon after entirely stopped. When the spring opened they fixed on Plymouth Rock (so called) for their permanent settlement. They were now more prosperous in whatever they undertook. Their number, to be sure, was reduced nearly one-half, and they could not count more than thirty-five or six.

"This year they built better habitations, cleared land, planted Indian corn and pumpkins, also a large garden in which were raised beets, carrots, parsnips, cabbage, etc.; likewise a large patch of turnips, all of which yielded them a plentiful harvest in the fall.

"Between one and two years from the time that these pilgrims landed on the Cape, the remainder of the Rev. Mr. Robertson's congregation crossed the ocean and joined them at Plymouth. They had left their beloved pastor behind, who had died of sickness in Holland.

"With this last party that arrived came the two brothers, that were of the same name as myself. The elder one was married, and the younger one married soon after he arrived in America.

"The mode of worship that was practiced by these Nonconformists was the same as practiced at the present time by Congregationalists and Presbyterians. At least the narrator has not been informed, or been able to discover, any essential difference.

"Our information will now be principally confined to the line of descendants from which the children of the younger brother, who is my ancestor, came. From about this time forward and for many years, emigrants were flocking into this country, not only by hundreds but by thousands, yearly, and were making settlements in various places along the coast, from Plymouth to Carolina, as also up the large rivers.

"The two brothers remained at Plymouth, but how many children each had I have not learnt, further than that the elder brother had many and the younger few, and that the younger had a grandson named Silas Phelps, and this Silas was my great grandfather.

"It is handed down to us that all along down to the present time, the descendants of the elder brother multiplied very fast, but not so with the descendants of the younger, who multiplied, but very slowly.

"From this it appears that the principal part of the Phelps' that are now in the country descended from the elder brother. The grandson mentioned above had a son named Jedediah who, after having a small family, together with a number of his neighbors, removed from Plymouth, through the wilderness, to Connecticut River, where they seated themselves down at a place called Northampton. This Jedediah Phelps was my grandfather.

"He lived several years at Northampton, when he sold his possessions and purchased a tract of land in the town of Lebanon, in what is now the State of Connecticut, on to which he removed with his family.

"He had three sons: Jacob, Jedediah, and Silas, which last was my father.

"Before my remembrance my grandfather and my two uncles died with lung fever. My grandmother lived several years longer, of whom I have some faint remembrance. My father survived and lived on the farm my grandfather gave him. He had six children—five sons and one daughter—Eliphalet, Anna, Silas, Jedediah, Joseph and Jacob. These all lived to have small families. The narrator has one son and two daughters; he has likewise fourteen grandchildren, and eleven great grandchildren. My father, mother, brothers and sisters have all gone to their long homes, and to add to my afflictions, God in his providence has seen fit to take from me my beloved wife, who died very suddenly on the 29th day of March, 1841.

"She was 85 years old, and had been my wife for about sixty-four years. My own age is nearly 90; yet I have great reason to be thankful that in some measure I retain my reason, and I am still able to read and write.

"It is my desire that as soon after my decease as may be, that this instrument of writing be handed over to my grandson, Jedediah Phelps, and my request to him is that he leave it with such one of his descendants as he may think proper; and if our descendants are faithful to the trust reposed in them, they will keep this instrument of writing going onward from one generation to another, by copying and re-copying down to the latest period of time.

"Town of Barre, Orleans county, State of New York, the 20th day of May, one thousand eight hundred and forty-four.

"JEDEDIAH PHELPS."

CHAPTER XXII.

SOME REMINISCENCES OF THE FAMILY IN ENGLAND AND AMERICA.

The following excerpts are taken from a letter dated at Vevay, Switzerland, October 17th, 1881, written to Rev. Alanson Phelps of Painesville, Ohio.

"It always gives me the greatest pleasure to afford any information in my power on the subject of my maternal ancestors,—the Phelps family, of Twining near Tewksbury,—a family now broken up, but to whose affection I owe everything, and whose representative I consider myself to be. They were not among the great of the land, but people of good standing and landed property, long established at Tewksbury and its environs as you may see from an excellent history of Tewksbury, now out of print, but of which I procured a copy for Judge Phelps.

"The oldest entry on the register of births at Tewksbury now extant is the baptism of James Phelps; among his descendants a dispersion seems to have occurred when some, including William Phelps, emigrated to the United States, then a British Colony, and another of the family

Edward, remained at home. In him continued the elder branch of the family and possession of the property.

"Certainly the original Coat of Arms was simply the black lion, of which I send you some impressions. I possess the Seal which is very simple but antique.

"A member of the family served under Cromwell and received a grant of land from him in Ireland, with probably a Coat of Arms, (I have seen it,) and his decendants occupy a high standing.

"Other branches went to Salisbury, and one of them was John Phelps, who, with Andrew Broughton, (buried in St. Martin's Church at Vevay,) held the office of clerk at the trial of Charles First, and his likeness may be seen on an old picture at the British Museum.

"In the parish of Twining near Tewksbury one of the hamlets bears the name of "Phelps," but I do not know how it passed out of the family.

"The entailed estate was at Twining, called 'Packrup House.'

"I was born there. My grandfather William Phelps had two sons, William and Frederick, with three daughters. The youngest daughter, Mary, my mother, alone had issue. My uncle William Law Phelps, the eldest son, being unmarried and in consideration of a sum of money, made an arrangement with his father whereby in accordance with the laws of England all entails may be cut off. This they did, and it was the ruin of the family, as well as the loss of the estate.

"On my grandfather's death disputes occurred in the family. It got into the Court of Chancery during my minority, and to make a long story short, some ten or twelve law suits were started among us until all was eaten out. *Sic transit gloria mundi*. I have been chaplain at this place for thirty years. I have six sons. My age is 67. Space fails me. I conclude with fraternal good wishes.

"Yours very sincerely,

"WILLIAM PHELPS PRIOR."

William Walter Phelps of New Jersey and Charles A. Phelps of Massachusetts have caused a memorial stone to be erected at the grave, in Vevay, Switzerland, of their ancestor John Phelps.

It bears the inscription on the following page.

IN MEMORIAM.

Of Him Who, Being with Andrew Broughton,
Joint Clerk of the Court
Which Tried and Condemned Charles the First
Of England,
Had Such Zeal to Accept the Full Responsibility,
Of His Act
That He Signed Each Record with His Full
Name,
JOHN PHELPS.
He Came to Vevay and Died, Like His Associates
Whose Memorials
Are About Us, An Exile in the Cause of Human
Freedom.
This Stone is Placed at the Request of
William Walter Phelps of New Jersey and
Charles A. Phelps of Massachusetts,
Descendants From Across The Seas.

The following excerpts are taken from an old letter of Mrs. Wyntop, no date given:

"Judge John Phelps, third generation from 'Auld William,' resided at Stafford Springs, Tolland County, Conn. It was natural, as the family had hailed from Staffordshire, England, for him to name the town 'Stafford,'

"Judge John Phelps married Mary Richardson, the only child of Lady Abigail Richardson of Scotland, a widow residing in the rural town of Suffield, a few miles from Windsor:

"Lady Richardson was a splendid and beautiful person, sat in a great square pew at church, and always carried a 'posie,' which was a bunch of flowers tied to a long stick with a blue ribbon.

"This, with a sprig of fennel, was always given to the favorite grandchild in meeting. She would not sanction the marriage of her accomplished young daughter of 15 to Mr. John Phelps, aged 19.

"This was the ostensible reason; others guessed her Scotch pride had something to do in the matter—her young, very beautiful and highly-toned daughter ought to command the very best match in the land.

"At this the maiden rebelled. She was shut up in her room until permission should be given for her release. The young people, however, managed well. The dwelling had a lean-to roof, which caused the windows in the rear to be low. 'Mammy Kitty,' a slave, was active in carrying notes to the distressed swain, and acted a clever part in the transaction.

"One moonlight evening after the village bell had tolled the hour of nine (bed-time) and the good mother was hushed in slumber, John comes, the bundles of clothing went down, then came the young girl, Mary, who cast herself into the arms of her lover.

"They went immediately to the parson, as had been previously arranged, where the nuptial knot was tied. After this he escorted his bride to his own home. It is affirmed that for six months they lived on pork and beans, corn and hasty pudding.

"The mother made the best of it, saying it was owing to the extreme youth of the parties that she opposed the marriage.

"She lived to see them surrounded with every earthly comfort, and her aspirations realized, and died at an old age.

"My mother always spoke of her as a stately personage. She (her name Abigail) was her favorite grandchild.

"Judge John Phelps died having an exalted name as a Christian gentleman. He was a friend of Washington. He was often solicited to enter public life in Philadelphia, but declined the excitement of its responsibilities and honor, and was happier in the retiracy of his family.

"He used his influence in his own State of Connecticut, where he won its honors and received its gratitude.

"For a number of years he represented the State in its General Assembly, and retired as one of its judges. His investment in his iron mines yielded him a large income. His daughters were fair and accomplished.

"They were educated in Boston at the only boarding school then in New England. Learning to play the piano was thought an uncommon accomplishment at that time. To obtain a thorough knowledge of it, it was thought necessary at each lesson to be accompanied by a flute and bass viol to preserve the time, and requiring three teachers instead of one.

"Esther, the eldest daughter of Judge John Phelps and Mary Richardson, married Elijah Austin, a merchant of New Haven. Mary, the second daughter, married Deacon Nathan Beers, and lived to great age, only lacking eighteen months of a century.

"Abigail Richardson (the youngest child) married Judge Isaac Mills, and died aged 83 years. Daniel Phelps lived in Connecticut. His son, Judge Phelps, of Painesville, Ohio, was greatly respected.

"His daughter, Mary Phelps, married her cousin, Peleg Phelps Sanford, son of Esther and her second husband. Timothy Phelps married Janet Broome. His second wife was Henrietta Broome, sister of Janet.

"Their father was commissioned by the British Crown as Governor of the American colonies. He was cousin of Sir Admiral Peter

Parker and Lord Elgin—nephew of William Pitt, Earl of Chatam."

To the courtesy of William Schuyler Moses, Esq., of San Francisco, Cal. (whose ancestors were cotemporaries of our ancestors in Windsor and its vicinity), the editor is under obligation for the following historical sketch of two relics of great antiquarian value, which have come down to him through his ancestors of "ye olden tyme."

As the readers of this book will readily see, Mr. Moses possesses an original mind, and is a man of scientific attainments as well:

"SAN FRANCISCO, June 26th, 1896.
"*Alanson H. Phelps, Esq.*

"DEAR SIR—Your request at our interview a few days since, that I should give you a history of a few heirlooms, that have been transmitted to me from my ancestors of 1640 and later, who were cotemporaries with your own from the early settlements at Canton, Simsbury, Barkhamstead and Hartford, to about the year 1808, will now be acceded to, so far as I am able to do. You must remember that in the two hundred and fifty years that have elapsed, much that is known to us now is largely traditional, as access to records, even if they were right, is difficult, and in most cases impossible; but in this case I have the articles to show.

"First—Is the copper spoon moulds, in

which were cast the leaden or pewter spoons used by the early settlers. In my own remembrance, over sixty years ago, it was the custom of my grandfather, on a stormy day, to gather up all the broken, bent and worn-out spoons, and with the big ladle at the old fire-place, cast anew the pewter spoons for the family use during the winter. These spoon moulds, family tradition says, were brought to Dorchester, Mass., by John Moses in 1632.

"Second—The calumet, or pipe of peace, is identical in shape and ornament with a cut of one on page 317 of a "Pictorial History of America," by John Frost, L.L. D., in print in Philadelphia, 1854.

"This pipe was possibly used at the signing of the deed to John Moses and George Abbet, by the Massacoe Chiefs Pacatoco, Pamatacount, and Youngcowet, on the 28th of June, 1648, when the above three chiefs of the Massacoes sold the lands of the town of Simsbury, Conn.

"The original of that deed I have seen and read, and it was at the old homestead as late as 1855, and as all bargains at that time with the Indians were always closed with a smoke of peace and good will, it is not impossible that this calumet was used at that time. *Or it is possible* that it came from a later period, viz., 1672 to 1675, when John Moses was a soldier in the King Philip war, where he lost two sons, Thomas aged 22 years, and William aged 19 years. After the death of King Philip, peace was made with the remnants of the Pequot tribe, and as John Moses was present then, the pipe may have come from them; at any rate I have known the pipe for over sixty-five years in our family. As I first remember it, it was a splendid specimen of laborious work. The stem was covered with feathers of many colors, and there was attached to it two long strings of shell wampum. It is my intention to restore its feather ornaments as I remember them nearly seventy years ago, and, if possible, also the wampum.

"I cannot, of course, tell which of the foregoing traditions may be the correct one, but it is certain the pipe has been in our family 225 or 250 years.

"The bowl of the pipe is made of a hard brown stone, and is about the size of the bowls of ordinary clay pipes now in use, except that the walls of the bowl are very much thicker than the modern clay pipes are.

"The stem is made of ash—a flat stem—being one and three-quarters of an inch in width, and three-eighths of an inch in thickness, and twenty-eight inches long.

"Addenda. I find that Timothy Moses, my great great grandfather, married, as his first wife, Sarah Phelps, who died September 12th, 1751.

"He was a man *much given to marriage*, for he afterward married three other wives (wonder what St. Peter said to him when he called at the outer gate?). I always thought there was some family tie between us, for I sometimes recognize in the family mutual characteristics.

"My father outlived *three* wives, and your brother has his *second*, and when I do anything that my conscience (what little I have) smites me for, I console myself with the thought, *that* is from Tim's *first wife*, and I know that when your brother does anything he is ashamed of, he is just as likely as not to charge it up to my account.

"I am as ever yours, partner in misfortune, superior in iniquity, and fellow-traveler on the road to eternity,

"WILLIAM SCHUYLER MOSES."

Mr. Moses also has another relic of the olden time that possesses great antiquarian interest, especially to the family of Phelps in general, in the form of an old *lease*, written on only one side of a sheet of paper (which he has permitted the editor to copy for this book), made and executed by Benjaman Phelps of Simsbury, Conn., to Thomas Phelps of the same place. The original of this old lease, written in the old-fashioned style of penmanship then in use, and with the appearance of having been written by Benjamin Phelps himself, from the similarity of the writing with his autograph, is sacredly preserved by Mr. Moses.

The lease is as follows:

"Know all men by these presents, that I, Benjamin Phelps of Simsbury, in the County of

Hartford, and Colony of Connecticut, for a valuble sum of money, to-wit, Two Pounds lawful money to me in hand paid received to my full satisfaction of Thomas Phelps of Simsbury aforesaid, Do Release, Remise and to Farm, Let unto him the said Thomas Phelps and to his heirs, and assigns, for and during the full term of Nine Hundred and Ninety-Nine years next ensuing, the one half of all the Mines, Minerals, Mettles and Oars of Mettles of what Nature, kind or quality whatsoever, that shall at any Time hereafter During said term be found in any part, or parcels, of land, which I have ever bought of him the said Thomas in the bounds of Simsbury in West Simsbury Society, with full Liberty for him the said Thomas, his heirs or Assigns, at any Time or Times During said Term, to Enter upon the Premises, to Digg, Search for, Sink Shafts, work and Separate any such Oars or Mettles, and with Teams and Carriages to carry away, all such Oars or Mettles, and Oars he or they shall find and Raise on said Land, Only reserving to myself, heirs and Assigns at my own cost and Labour, to carry on the One half of the business of Raising Oars, &c, as aforesaid for my own and their profit and use. To have and to hold the said premises and Released Premises with the appurtenances thereof unto him the said Thomas Phelps his heirs and Assigns, without let, suit, claim, henderance or Molestation from the said Benjamin Phelps my heirs Executors or Administrators,

or any other person or persons from by or under me. In witness whereof I have hereunto set my hand and seal the 24th day of April, 1769.
"Benjamin Phelps.
"Signed, Sealed and Delived
"in Presence of
"Josiah Case,
"Abraham Case."

CHAPTER XXIII.

CONCLUSION.

The labor of the editor is done. To the best of his ability he has compiled and arranged in as clear and concise a form as practicable, with the facilities to be obtained on the Pacific Coast, and yet he has, as it were, only skirted the border land of mystery surrounding the lives of the first five generations enumerated in this book. He is conscious—supremely conscious—that there are many delinquencies in it, but he is confident that the records here enrolled will be useful in the future to many of the name of Phelps yet unborn.

Before he writes "the end," he wishes to draw a picture, which may possibly come true sometime in the coming centuries:

In the year 2196 of the Christian Era, one day a man of middle age carelessly sauntered into a large and commodious public library in the populous City of Tucson, Arizona.

He was seeking he knew not what, and entered the library, as the day was very warm, to find a cool and shady retreat. He entered one of the alcoves where were stored the most neglected and worn-out books of the whole library—books that had seen better days—some in tattered covers showing hard and continuous usage, others so useless in themselves that no one had ever handled them except to get them out of the way.

He stepped up to the shelves and began to look at the old books of various kinds. Among other books which he took down was one that had the appearance of very great age; it was covered with the dust of many years, the binding was frayed and in a dilapidated condition. He examined it casually, but with no particular interest; opened it and saw the title page, reading, "Genealogy of One Branch of the Family of George Phelps."

He had never seen or even heard of the book before. He turned over a few of its leaves and saw the Chapter headed, "The Line of the Family."

He began to be interested in it, as he was a descendant on his mother's side (her maiden name having been Harriet Aurelia Phelps) of the Phelps Family long identified with the great State of California.

Seeking an easy seat he pored over the old book with increasing interest from beginning to end, and ere he had finished it he was convinced that at last he had found the "missing link" which he had been in search of many years, that would enable him to prove that he was the only surviving heir of a grand uncle of his mother, who had died in 2155 and had left a large and valuable estate in California for which no heirs had ever been able to prove their right of inheritance.

He took the book to the librarian and requested that he might carry it away with him. As the book never before in the history of the library had been called for—or at least in the memory of the then librarian, who was an elderly man who had spent nearly all his life in the service of the library—the request was readily granted, with the condition, however, that it must be returned within two months from date. This he agreed to do, and, giving a receipt, he was permitted to take it away. He took it at once to an attorney who was well versed in solving the riddles so often concealed in old wills, and who also had a profound knowledge of the law relating to escheated estates, and, showing him the book, stated to him that he believed that if he could get the matter of his great grand uncle's estate re-opened in court, that he would be able with it to prove his kinship to his uncle, and that he would be declared his lawful heir, and be entitled to the estate.

Together they went over the book. Many passages in it brought smiles of derision to their lips, because of the crude and uncultured style in which the poor old editor had sought to clothe the historical parts of the narrative.

But they were forced to admit that the records themselves—the manner in which they were set forth in the book, were clear and perspicacious and bore internal evidence of being really *authentic*.

The lawyer was impressed with the strength of the case as presented in the old book, and agreed to assume charge of the case, and would endeavor to have it brought before the proper court in the State of California. In due time this was done—the case having been assigned to the Probate Department of the Superior Court in the City and County of Oakland in the State of California, in which County the major portion of the landed estate was situated. The case was brought to trial—the plaintiff appearing with seven of the ablest attorneys as counsel, practicing in the courts of the State; the case was presented to the judge in open court; the old book, the principal evidence the plaintiff had to establish his case, was offered in evidence —was carefully examined by the learned attorneys representing the State and by the distinguished judge on the bench, and after a full and exhaustive hearing of the whole matter, the judge handed down a decision that the plaintiff, Asa Hosmer Austin, was the rightful and legal heir of his Great Grand Uncle William Eliphalet Phelps of Milpitas, California, and gave him the estate.

This fanciful picture, showing what may possibly happen in the years to come, illustrates the necessity for the faithful keeping and the preservation of family records, and is introduced here to show to the descendants of our family the utility of the custom of faithfully preserving their own family records.

The editor commits this book to the descendants of the family wherever they may live, for preservation, and to the care of the Infinite Father.

THE END.

THE PRINTER BEGAN HIS WORK ON THIS BOOK IN THE MONTH OF SEPTEMBER MDCCCXCVII AND FINISHED IT IN THE MONTH OF OCTOBER FOLLOWING. OF THIS BOOK TWO HUNDRED COPIES ONLY EXIST WHICH ARE FOR PRIVATE CIRCULATION. THE WORK WAS DONE IN SAN FRANCISCO AT THE PRINTING SHOP OF THE E. D. TAYLOR COMPANY.

www.ingramcontent.com/pod-product-compliance
Lightning Source LLC
Chambersburg PA
CBHW020824230426
43666CB00007B/1088